My Not So Brilliant Dating Career

by

C C Blooms

Copyright 2025 © C C Blooms

All rights reserved. No part of this publication may be reproduced, stored in a retrieval system, or transmitted in any form or by any means, electronic, mechanical, photocopying, recording, or otherwise, without the prior permission of the author and copyright owner of this book.

For my dear friend Charlotte, who always spoke the wisest of words. You'll be pleased to know I finally listened.

To my most favourite people in my world - Mum, Dad, Sis, Brother-in-law and nephews - always my biggest supports.

Continued champagne raising of glasses to Alison, Samantha and Andrew for the countless times I've told you I was going on a date and then calling the next day to tell you it was a disaster.

Thanks to Tiff whose path the universe put in front of me to cross to help me realise my potential.

To Marla from the New York Book Editors who encouraged me to persist.

To Jacqui who had the patience to help make this book legible.

To anyone brave enough to read this, I am grateful.

All names have been changed to protect the innocent, all stories are made up.

Contents

Chapter 1: Kinder Karma 1
Chapter 2: Kiss Chasey 7
Chapter 3: Hubba Bubba 11
Chapter 4: Year 9 Dancing Class 15
Chapter 5: Asthma Attack 20
Chapter 6: Year 12 Formal 24
Chapter 7: Tooheys New 28
Chapter 8: Just Do It 33
Chapter 9: Get Used To This 36
Chapter 10: Identity Crisis 41
Chapter 11: Never Mix a Magpie with a Cockatoo 45
Chapter 12: Wrong Guy 49
Chapter 13: Pearl Earrings 53
Chapter 14: Coaster-man 57
Chapter 15: Driza-Bone 63
Chapter 16: Beached Whale 68
Chapter 17: Salty Ol' Sea Dog 71
Chapter 18: The Mauler 77
Chapter 19: Nose Dripper 82
Chapter 20: Stock Market Crash 85
Chapter 21: Skinny Runner 91
Chapter 22: The Ghoster 98
Chapter 23: It's Not a Movie 100
Chapter 24: Sweaty Hands Flatmate 105
Chapter 25: Sprung Nurse 109
Chapter 26: Portrait 115

Chapter 27: Speed Dating Situation #1 120
Chapter 28: Fired on a Boat 126
Chapter 29: Driving Range 130
Chapter 30: Milk pudding PT 133
Chapter 31: Anyone for Pimms? 137
Chapter 32: The red G-Banger 141
Chapter 33: My name isn't Julie 144
Chapter 34: Horse Race Commentator 148
Chapter 35: Whimpering at a Wine Bar 151
Chapter 36: Corporate Surfer 155
Chapter 37: The Arborist 160
Chapter 38: Family Jewels 164
Chapter 39: Carbon Tax Lawyer 168
Chapter 40: I think I'm in Hell-i-tosis 173
Chapter 41: Speed Dating Attempt #2 178
Chapter 42: Brainstrust 183
Chapter 43: Textationship 187
Chapter 44: Expensive Dinner 191
Chapter 45: Four 195
Chapter 46: Tea Leaves 201
Chapter 47: Nostril Licker 204
Chapter 48: Coach vs Couch 208
Chapter 49: Cop That 212
Chapter 50: Pomm Fizzle 216
Chapter 51: Not so Magic Mike 220
Chapter 52: Barry White 224
Chapter 53: Fast Food 227
Chapter 54: Tinder-National 231
Chapter 55: Heart Attack 235

Chapter 1

Kinder Karma

Penny Curtis
To: Stephanie Thompson
Re: I've worked it out!

I've worked it out!

Stephanie Thompson
To: Penny Curtis
Re: I've worked it out!

Um…it's pretty early and I haven't had my coffee. But I'm intrigued, tell me what have you worked out?

Penny Curtis
To: Stephanie Thompson
Re: I've worked it out!

Why I'm single!!

Stephanie Thompson
To: Penny Curtis
Re: I've worked it out!

And why is this?

Penny Curtis
To: Stephanie Thompson
Re: I've worked it out!

Stems back to kindergarten! Remember what happened in the treehouse?

Stephanie Thompson
To: Penny Curtis
Re: I've worked it out!

W.H.A.T ? ! ? ! You are mad...

When I was in kinder, I may have accidentally pushed a kid out of the treehouse, and he may have accidentally broken his arm. And that's why I believe I am having difficulty meeting the true love of my life. That's why I'm single.

It's called karma.

I never intentionally set out to break his arm. I don't think I am a violent person, well, not at five years of age anyway. It all just seemed to happen in a blur.

Stephanie and I were being chased by two boys, Tom and Jerry. We decided to escape from them by climbing up the treehouse. It was only a few metres off the ground, but at the age of five it felt like we were climbing a mountain. Out of breath, we reached the platform, only to discover that Tom and Jerry were already there, waiting for us.

Standing over us, Jerry called me names while Tom acted as his backup, throwing a few *yeah*s at us. Stephanie and I scrambled to our feet and tried desperately to fend them off. I felt my face getting redder as Jerry, who was awfully close to me, kept spitting saliva as he yelled. I don't know what overcame me, but in one fell swoop, I pushed with all my might into Jerry's chest. Jerry lost his balance awkwardly and flew out the treehouse window.

This was definitely not the outcome I was expecting. We all froze, except Jerry, who was in free fall. I looked aghast at Stephanie for support, and then we both looked at Tom. I think we were all in shock. I can still hear Jerry screaming uncontrollably from the ground below. In a flurry, we looked out the window and saw the commotion. Teachers were running everywhere, kids were screaming, and poor Jerry was wailing and holding his arm. It was chaos.

Jerry's arm was broken, and I admit I had something to do with it, but I'd also like to point out that the way he flew out the window wasn't ideal for landing on the tanbark below. He should have rolled or made some attempt for less impact when he landed, in my opinion, as it wasn't really *that* far to fall. If he had rolled, he would have been less likely to break anything.

All I remember is being called into the principal's office and seeing my parents in there. Suffice to say I got in BIG trouble.

Fast forward twenty years, and after so many horrendous dates, I began thinking that perhaps this unfortunate incident was the reason or my karma for not finding 'the one'.

There was only one way to find out: track down Jerry and ask him for forgiveness. Perhaps then the curse would then be lifted.

I tracked Jerry down in no time, thanks to social media. At first, Jerry had no idea who I was. However, after a light-hearted joke about breaking his arm in kindergarten, he quickly remembered the incident and took a swipe back at me, asking if I wanted to break his arm again. Not funny, Jerry. I explained my predicament, and he seemed quite empathetic to me.

After a while, he told me the truth about why he and Tom were teasing me – it was because he liked me. I couldn't believe it - we could have been childhood sweethearts! Jerry said that he felt he did deserve to get pushed and that he actually lost his balance and fell awkwardly. The sill of the window ledge was broken, so it didn't hold his fall, hence he went flying out the window.

In the end, he was laughing and trying to tell me that he forgave me and had never held a grudge. We chattered a little longer, caught up on each other's lives and agreed to keep in touch.

Penny Curtis
To: Stephanie Thompson
Re: I've worked it out!

He's forgiven me!

Stephanie Thompson
To: Penny Curtis
Re: I've worked it out!

Hallelujah! What did he say?

Penny Curtis
To: Stephanie Thompson
Re: I've worked it out!

He confessed he had a crush on me, but all is forgiven now. Can you believe it? I think this has lifted my singledom!

Stephanie Thompson
To: Penny Curtis
Re: I've worked it out!

Is it too early for a celebratory champagne? I can meet you downstairs in 15? I just have to wait until the GM walks out to go to his meeting.
Tell me though, more importantly, is Jerry still single?

Penny Curtis
To: Stephanie Thompson
Re: I've worked it out!!

It's never too early for a drink see you in a jiffy. But no, he's not single, married with three kids.

Stephanie Thompson
To: Penny Curtis
Re: I've worked it out!!

Brill, see you in a sec. Now that there's no karma we have to get you back out there and only break hearts not arms!

Although I thought this incident had paved the way to my freedom to find '*the one*, I began to reflect on other incidents that perhaps were the reason as to why my singledom had not yet been lifted......

Chapter 2

KISS CHASEY

Penny Curtis
To: Stephanie Thompson
Re: Could this be a reason?

Might be over thinking it… but perhaps the breaking arm incident was one of many incidents which all add up, like a black cat has nine lives or something?

Stephanie Thompson
To: Penny Curtis
Re: Could this be a reason?

Oh darl, I think you need to relax, you've been forgiven. What possibly could be worse than a broken arm?

Penny Curtis
To: Stephanie Thompson
Re: Could this be a reason?

No, you're right, maybe I am overthinking it a little. But the incident in primary school when we played Kiss Chasey might just be some additional salt to the wound?

Stephanie Thompson
To: Penny Curtis
Re: Could this be a reason?

The only salt needed is the one on your wrist when I meet you after work on Friday for Tequila shots! In the meantime, think about what you want to do about this Kiss Chasey incident.

I couldn't stop thinking about my behaviour during this particular Kiss Chasey incident. I partly blame Dad, as the weekend before, he had been teaching my sister and me how to catch birds in some concoction of a cage he had built. And that had given me an idea.

I wasn't the skinniest of kids, nor was I particularly fast over one hundred meters, so you can appreciate I had to be slightly more strategic if I was going to catch the love of my life. Even if I didn't know who that was.

So, after years of torment holding the ends of the elastics for the rest of the skinny bitches, one of them finally asked me to participate in their game of Kiss Chasey, a demoralizing game in itself if you are not quick or are hit with the ugly stick. Still, I felt I was quick strategically, thanks to Dad and his bird cage strategy.

On this particular afternoon, I had been told whom I was allowed to chase down (sounds barbaric) and decided that this was my moment to kiss the only guy no one wanted, which suited me as it was clearly evident no one wanted me. I made a few flabby attempts to grab Philip's hand or, better yet, his jumper, but he was far too quick for this non-shrinking violet.

Knowing there wasn't much time left before the recess bell went for the afternoon classes, I decided to adopt my new strategy involving…the boys' toilets. I'm not proud of myself, but it was my only hope!

Philip had run into the toilets, so I hovered quietly just outside. When I heard the loo flush, I was ready to pounce. Philip came out, completely unaware I was there. I grabbed him and launched in to kiss him, got the back of his ear lobe and copped a mouthful of his hair. And he got me too, but unfortunately, it wasn't a kiss. He squarely punched me in the guts and screamed some awful words at me as he ran off.

Although my stomach was hurting from Philip's punch, my heart was pounding with pride that I'd strategically managed to kiss Philip, and without too much of a chase.

Penny Curtis
To: Stephanie Thompson
Re: Could this be a reason

I've had a good think about it, and I now realise that the Kiss Chasey incident wasn't as bad as I thought. His mother punished me in the end, so I believe we were even-stevens and therefore I don't think I need to track Philip down for forgiveness.

Stephanie Thompson
To: Penny Curtis
Re: Could this be a reason?

Oh yes, I remember Philip's mum grabbing you after school in front of everyone and bellowing how you'd attacked Philip. I think all is forgiven. All these 'incidents' are merely speed humps in your journey and aren't reflective as to why you're still single.
Men are just dicks. Except our dads, of course.

Penny Curtis
To: Stephanie Thompson
Re: Could this be a reason?

No, you're right, you always are. I'll kiss that goodbye and move on!

Stephanie Thompson
To: Penny Curtis
Re: Could this be a reason?

Excellent! Meet you at 6pm at The Mint for a few Tequila shots.

CHAPTER 3

HUBBA BUBBA

Penny Curtis
To: Stephanie Thompson
Re: Chewy in ya boot

I've got it !!

Stephanie Thompson
To: Penny Curtis
Re: Chewy in ya boot

Got what? Bubble gum stuck on your new $800 Tony Biancos?

Penny Curtis
To: Stephanie Thompson
Re: Chewy in ya boot

No, and as if I would spend that much on shoes! No, I was out last night for dinner with friends from tennis and across the restaurant was Ken Barrington?! And he didn't even acknowledge me when I waved at him....has to be a sign.

Stephanie Thompson
Penny Curtis
Re: Chewy in ya boot

You know I love you dearly, but today's not the day to be all cryptic on me as I am very hungover... who is Ken Barrington and where have I got chewing gum?

Ken Barrington was the brother of Lisa, a school friend of mine whom I also went horse riding with on the weekends. Ken was a few years older and was hot in my book. Whenever I went back to Lisa's after riding, Ken would help us unload the car. He was so lovely. However, at school Ken pretended he didn't know who I was, which I thought was particularly strange.

One hot summer weekend after riding, when Lisa and I were in her pool, I confessed to Lisa that I liked her brother. She teased me for a while but then encouraged me to tell Ken. A little while later, Ken joined us in the pool, but I acted all stupid and couldn't pluck up the courage to tell him I liked him.

The following week I bumped into Ken in the tuckshop queue while waiting to collect my lunch order. I froze because Ken never spoke to me at school. He said that Lisa had told him that I fancied him and that he thought that was cool. However, I needed to do something for him before he considered 'us'.

"Anything!" I exclaimed.

Ken said he wanted me to buy him a pack of grape Hubba Bubba chewing gum every week until he made up his mind that I could be his girlfriend. I couldn't believe my luck. I couldn't even recall picking up my tuckshop order that day and skipped all the way home after school, pretty happy with myself.

The reality check hit home on Thursday morning when Mum took my sister and me shopping because not only was the allowance mum gave us for helping her with the shopping not enough to cover a packet of Hubba Bubba, but them Mum said I wasn't allowed to buy chewing gum full stop.

I was in a pickle. How would I buy the love of my life his weekly packet of grape Hubba Bubba without Mum finding out?

I didn't know it then, but I went into entrepreneurial mode. I told mum I didn't want to put the money she gave me towards a milky way bar after helping her but instead wanted to save my money. I think she nearly crashed the Safeway trolley into the lady in front of her. Mum beamed at me, proud of her youngest daughter. Little did she know what I was saving for.

I scrimped and saved and asked for extra chores; my parents were flabbergasted. When I had enough saved that week, I'd sneak into the milk bar not far from school, buy a packet of Hubba Bubba, and then skip merrily to school, find Ken and hand it to him like he was a king.

This went on for weeks, and although I still liked Ken, I was resenting all the additional chores I was undertaking and not saving any money for myself or missing out on my milky way, but I didn't think of the weight loss and the non-holed teeth in the longer commitment. Thankfully it all came to quite a drastic conclusion.

I confronted Ken and told him this was the last packet of grape Hubba Bubba I was going to provide as I thought it had gone on long enough. Six months! He had the audacity to tell me that Cheryl was supplying him with strawberry Hubba Bubba, and he preferred that over grape flavoured gum. I couldn't believe it. I was flabbergasted.

Unfortunately, the following weekend when horse riding with Lisa, my horse was spooked, and I fell off, was knocked unconscious and fractured my skull. Fortunately, when I was better, Ken thought that he had had something to do with this incident and asked me to forgive him and gave back some money for all the packs of grape variety Hubba Bubba I bought him.

Stephanie Thompson
To: Penny Curtis
Re: Chewy in ya boot

I think overall that was quite drastic to go give yourself a fractured skull just because Keno like strawberry flavoured Hubba Bubba. Besides, a man has to eat…just joking!

Chapter 4

Year 9 Dancing Class

Penny Curtis
To: Stephanie Thompson
Re: He's no Fred Astaire

Tell me something, what were they thinking when they decided Year 9 dancing class was the best idea under the sun?

Stephanie Thompson
To: Penny Curtis
Re: He's no Fred Astaire

I'm with you, it was torturous, only bad memories of that whole experience!

Penny Curtis
To: Stephanie Thompson
Re: He's no Fred Astaire
I mean it's not as if we're going through enough as it was back then. Puberty for starters.

Stephanie Thompson
To: Penny Curtis
Re: He's no Fred Astaire

And the rest. I mean, we were still developing, and I didn't know if I was a boy or a girl in my looks at that stage. Not to mention the acne. I'll never forget that Friday night, though, with that horrendous guy you got to dance with, everyone was told to avoid him, but you were too nice and ended up dancing the night with him.

Dancing class: the hype around it was ridiculous. Even from a girls' school perspective, it went beyond normality. Don't get me wrong, I liked to look pretty, but I also liked wearing jeans and a t-shirt. The circus around the outfits was deplorable. One girl used to buy a dress, leave the tag on, wear it that night to dancing class then return it to the shop the next day. I used to look at her every Friday night in awe, thinking how lucky she was to have a new dress every week while the rest of us wore the same outfit. I found out later that she was caught by the shop and charged by Police.

I wore something that made me look like I was from an Amish clan (no offence, but you get the picture). I was also on my second round of braces because the first attempt didn't work, so the dentist thought I needed more drama in my mouth – think railway-track silver with blue bands on diagonals all over. When I spoke, which wasn't rare, I may have spat accidentally.

My T-zone was looking a little like the plague because I had acne, and my best friend had told me to use a foam-like product that I applied to the affected area – it felt like my skin was burning off. Man, it stung! Yet I continued to use it, and my acne continued to get worse. Hence, I wore make-up for my first dancing class. Boy, did I cake that on – so much so that, because there was heating in the assembly hall, make-up would drip down my face and by the end of the night, acne face would re-appear.

To top it off, there was the hairstyle. With absolutely no creative talent to make my hair look trendy, I decided to use my best friend's hair crimper and gel. Bad mistake. Think the 1980s with leg warmers, frizzed-up mullet. Firstly, here's a trick – don't put the crimper too close to your skull, or you'll burn yourself. This happened on a regular basis. When I accidentally hit my scalp and felt the burn, I'd react and move, and burn another part of my head. What's that saying, no pain no gain? So, I'd push through. After the scalding hair-crimping, I'd apply the gel. Again, not my forte. I'd put a scoop into the palm of my hands and run it through my burnt mane. It would just flop to the side of my face, so I looked like a grease ball with burnt crimped bits at the back.

Clearly, as the bell of the ball, I'd be the first to be selected to dance. It was the most shameful low-life way to shove your confidence further down the toilet. All the boys lined up on one side of the room and the girls on the other. If it were me, I would've blindfolded everyone, and you just got paired up with the first person in line. But no, these whack jobs of teachers thought of the clever confidence-depleting version instead. Boys selected a girl. So, all the hot-looking guys made a beeline for the hot chicks then all the ugly ducklings slowly got chosen. I was the ugly duckling, three-quarters of the way through, which wasn't so bad because at least I got selected.

Unfortunately, it was by Fred, the guy all my friends had warned me not to dance with.

Fred was like a male version of me. Sweaty palms, acne (worse than mine), braces (but not kamikaze blue elastic bands), bad hair, and an outfit that looked like a hand-me-down. I was thinking we were a perfect match! Plus, neither of us knew how to dance.

Little did I know that he thought he was Fred Astaire. I tried to listen to the dance instructor, but Fred decided he knew more. Then he told me I was wearing too much make-up and that maybe next time I shouldn't use gel. Thankfully, the music started, and we tried our first dance move – unsuccessfully. I looked down at his feet – they were huge! No wonder I couldn't manoeuvre my feet between or around his. But Fred was quick to tell me off for tripping over his feet. He said I was the clumsiest person he'd ever met.

Another tip from the instructor with Fred's commentary over the top. Another unsuccessful move with me tripping over Fred's feet. Another look of disgust from Fred followed a comment about my outfit. He said if I lifted my game in the outfit stakes, I might be more appealing to the male species. Gees thanks, Fred, my confidence has gone from minus two to minus ten. I kept looking at the clock when we whirled past it. One hour to go.

The instructor selected a couple to demonstrate to the class how to perform the final manoeuvre – a confusing combination with a weird-looking twirl on the end of it. When the teacher's pets could hardly carry it off, the rest of us had a chuckle. I was still laughing when I turned to face Fred. He put his arm up to his face and shouted for me to close my mouth as no one needed to see that train wreck. It tipped me over the edge.

I smiled more.

"Shut your mouth!" he snapped.

But I kept smiling my railway tracks at him. When his feet kept getting in the way, I decided to stand on them. At one point, we both fell over his feet. He was mortified and flew off the handle, calling me pathetic. Thankfully the instructor could see what was going on and came over and— wait for it— gave Fred instructions, while I smiled encouragingly at Fred with my biggest cheesy grin.

Once Fred had collected his thoughts, he grabbed my sweaty hands, and we were off again with the music. He could barely look at me, smiling up at him. Every now and then, he couldn't help himself and would make a derogatory comment toward me. I thought he was taking this far too seriously, to be honest, unless he was hoping to become one of those professional ballroom dancers – God help his partner.

Fred was becoming agitated. Thankfully, it was nearly home time, and everyone's parents had arrived and were gleefully watching our performance. We were leading up to the final dance move with the convoluted twirl, with Fred spinning me like a rag doll and missing steps, when on the last move, he twirled me so hard I couldn't stop. I reached out to grab his hand for him to pull me in for the finish, but Fred decided this was his moment not to hold out his hand. I flew backwards, tripped over his foot, and landed temple first on the corner of a metal seat. Fred just stood there.

The instructor and the deputy principal came rushing over. I had knocked myself out and was bleeding from the head. An ambulance arrived and took me off to the hospital.

I asked the Doctor for a certificate to say I never had to attend dancing class ever again.

He signed it.

CHAPTER 5

ASTHMA ATTACK

Penny Curtis
To: Stephanie Thompson
Re: Does this count?

How about the way I treated that poor bloke who took me for a run?

Stephanie Thompson
To: Penny Curtis
Re: Does this count?

I'm a bit foggy, only because I've been out for a long lunch ….but if I recall he wasn't 100% honest with you?

Penny Curtis
To: Stephanie Thompson
Re: Does this count?

You're always on a 'long lunch'…but yes, you are right

Stephanie Thompson
To: Penny Curtis
Re: Does this count?

I guess you ended up being even?

Stephanie could be right. The poor bugger didn't know what hit him.

I was at the movies with a friend and her brother when we bumped into someone they knew. His name was Martin, and he was tall, handsome and very fit-looking.

Unbeknown to me, he asked my friend's brother if he thought I'd be interested in him, and the next minute I received a text from him. I was flattered. Martin was polite and suggested we go on a date.

I had recently got involved in triathlons and was enjoying the training aspect, so something overcame me, and I suggested that our first date could be a run. Only, I was no runner. Any race photographer snap revealed that I looked more like Cliff Young going backwards – my feet never left the ground.

But Martin was keen. Too keen. I didn't pick up on this, unfortunately. Mum answered the door, and there was Martin in his running shorts, singlet top and fancy spiked running shoes, while I rocked up in my long Nike leggings and Nike long sleeve running top as if I were in Alaska.

"You sure you won't be too hot?" Mum said in passing. I brushed Mum off, what would she know?

I was too besotted to notice Martin's outfit – I was just so happy to be on a date with a good-looking bloke who was fit and could potentially be my date for my Year 12 formal. Pity, because it would have given me some serious clues.

We weren't even out of the front gate when he started jogging on the spot, doing funny leg kicks and side jumps. I began to jog (more of a fast walk), and Martin jogged beside me. As we continued, I felt myself getting out of breath and really hot (I should've listened to Mum) while Martin was having a normal non-huffing and non-puffing conversation with me, looking like he was taking it easy without even a sweat. Then he suggested we lift the pace – pftfft, of course, this is just the warm-up for me (liar). Panic set in.

Not five minutes in, I felt like I was going to burst. I could hardly breathe, my legs felt like we were going at a hundred miles an hour, my arms weren't in sync with my legs, I was one big exploding mess. Meanwhile, Martin was trotting along, still chatting. I couldn't reply to his questions, I could only grunt, and even that was an effort. I was beetroot red. It's a wonder no one in the neighbourhood dialled 000.

But instead of stopping and confessing, I went into 'let's make something up so I feel better about myself' mode. I tumbled to the pavement and exclaimed between faked gasps:

"You…" gasp "go…" gasp "on…" gasp "without me." Gasp. "I…" gasp "have…" gasp "asthma."

Martin wasn't sure what just hit him, but in a gentleman-like fashion, he crouched down next to me to rub my back and console me. He scolded me for not telling him I had asthma as he wouldn't have picked up the pace so much and suggested we could have walked instead. He helped me up, and we walked back to my house— where Mum met us at the door with one eyebrow raised as Martin explained how sorry he was he didn't know I suffered from asthma.

Before Mum could say anything, I jumped in and asked Martin if he'd like some water.

Stephanie Thompson
To: Penny Curtis
Re: Does this count?

It doesn't count, because he didn't provide a full disclosure either

Penny Curtis
To: Stephanie Thompson
Re: Does this count?

You're right! Even though I lied about my asthma, I found out later that he actually qualified for the Commonwealth Games in the 800m sprint.

Chapter 6

Year 12 Formal

Penny Curtis
To: Stephanie Thompson
Re: Final Formal Frenzy

I'll never live down end of year 12 formal!

Stephanie Thompson
To: Penny Curtis
Re:

No, unfortunately that one will go down in history, I'm actually not sure what you were thinking? You were so organised, had it together then it was as if you'd lost your shit completely at the last-minute right before your final moment….

Penny Curtis
To: Stephanie Thompson
Re: Final Formal Frenzy

It wasn't one of my finer moments

Life had just caught up with me. I'd been so busy with my school commitments and studying for end-of-year exams that I left what I had actually wanted to focus on until the very last minute. And boy, did I pay for it.

"If we don't start shopping for material for your dress, you won't have one. Or worse, you'll have to wear your dress from last year," said Mum.

To ease Mum's stress, I told her that I trusted her. I said I was happy for her to find a dress pattern and material and to organise the dressmaker. My sister was in hysterics. She shook her head in disbelief – but how bad could Mum's idea of a year 12 formal dress be?

At a BBQ at a girlfriend's house the weekend before the formal, I started talking to a guy named was Andrew. By the end of the night, I was planning our wedding (in my head). A few days later, I asked my girlfriend to ask her sister if Andrew would be my date for the formal. I got a yes.

There were lots of school commitments leading up to the Friday night formal. I was running around, making speeches, shaking hands, bearing gifts and trying to finish an assessment. Mum tried taking my measurements as I still hadn't had a dress-fitting, but apparently, the dress was underway.

I had made no contact with Andrew. All he knew was the address of the before-drinks at another girlfriend's house.

On the day of the formal, I had to make a speech at a church function for some former teachers, hot foot it across to a sporting event where I was to present a trophy and then attend an afternoon tea (no alcohol) for some of our school's donors. When I got home, my sister had the crimper ready, and Mum had my dress ready to throw on. I was running very late.

With my hair and make-up done, I looked like a drag queen (which I think was my sister's intention). Mum helped me into the dress, which looked like an inflatable toy you'd put in a pool and in techno-colour dream colours to match my drag queen look. It felt a little tight. In fact, a lot tight! But I sucked my guts in and jumped in a taxi to the pre-drinks party.

As I got out of the taxi, I heard a ripping noise. The side part of my dress starting under my arm had ripped straight down the seam! Whoops. Scurrying up to my girlfriend's house, her mum answered the door, and she could see the terror on my face.

"What's happened?"

I turned to the side and lifted up my arm.

"Easily fixed. Come through to my room, I'll sew it up quickly. It'll be fine."

After three attempts at sewing the relatively large gap, we made the decision to safety pin it.

"It's very in," she said reassuringly. "I've seen many dresses with safety pins as an actual feature." Oh terrific, I'll be 'in' then.

Keeping my arm as close as I could to my side and holding my glass of champagne close to me, I mingled. Eventually, a girlfriend brought over Andrew.

"You remember Andrew from my BBQ? He's your date for tonight."

"Yes, of course. How are you, Andrew?" I said, awkwardly. I reached my hand out to shake his, and as I did, the sleeve of my dress exploded open. Ignoring it, I kept talking while he stared.

"Is everything okay with your dress?" Andrew asked.

"Oh yes, this is on trend with the fashions nowadays." He didn't look very impressed.

Not much was said between us in the taxi on the way to the function room. I was too busy trying to remember my speech, not to mention keeping my dress expulsions to a minimum. I wriggled out of the cab so I wouldn't rip another part of my dress and waddled into the function room.

Unfortunately for Andrew, I was dragged away in every direction by the teachers. I'd look back at the table, and Andrew would be sitting by himself, eating the dinner roll off his side plate. Every time I tried to sit next to him I was dragged off somewhere else.

Then the lights went down, and I was introduced. As I walked up to the stage and started my speech to my fellow year 12s, I couldn't help but notice Andrew was eating the rest of my main course. I continued, but halfway through, Andrew wiped his mouth with his serviette, pushed his chair out, got up and left the building. Never to return for the evening.

I finished my speech and sat down next to Steph.

"Next time, I'd come by myself," she said.

Thanks for stating the obvious Steph. What a disaster of a night. That poor guy. I did try contact him to apologise but heard nothing back from him, which is totally understandable.

Chapter 7

TOOHEYS NEW

Penny Curtis
To: Stephanie Thompson
Re: I feel like a Tooheys

I never thought I'd say this, but I believe this holiday romance beer friend was the one.

Stephanie Thompson
To: Penny Curtis
Re: I feel like a Tooheys

Well, it might have been, but I'd have disowned you by now as that brand of beer, or any beer for that matter, is for bogans!

Penny Curtis
To: Stephanie Thompson
Re: I feel like a Tooheys

He would have matured like I have and now sip on martinis. And besides, it wasn't just any Tooheys. He was a Tooheys red man.

Take me back to that summer at the beach, our first taste of freedom.

We'd finished Year 12, no more exams, and in my case, hopefully, fewer pimples and reduced fat around my guts. A few of us had decided to head off to the beach for a week. One of the girls' boyfriends and his mates were also heading up. Everyone was excited to be there.

On the first day, we all headed off to the beach. We read books, laughed, popped in and out of the water and re-applied the sunscreen – and repeated this ritual all day until the sunset. That evening we meet up for some pre-dinner drinks.

And there he was… a god-like human specimen. I don't think I've ever seen anyone as good-looking. I couldn't talk, and I avoided him like the plague. Lucky for me, there was no way this guy would talk to me with him an Adonis and me a mere mortal. A few girls talked with him, but I would only sneak the occasional glance. My face burnt beetroot red every time.

We repeated the beach ritual by day and, at night, caught up for drinks. One night, we decided to head down to the local open-air movie. As we were gathering, the Adonis introduced himself to me. I looked around, startled. Clearly, he's made a mistake, why would he want to talk with me? Awkwardly, I murmured out a 'hello' and picked up my walking pace. He laughed at me, picked up his stride and walked next to me.

"You like swimming in the ocean?" he asked.

Why is he talking to *me*? Trying to act cool wasn't my greatest attribute, so instead of replying to him, I walked into a tree.

The Adonis began helping me off the ground and looking at the incredibly big bruise starting to form above my right eye.

"Are you ok?" he asked.

"Of course," I exclaimed as if I do this type of thing all the time.

Once we were in the movies, the Adonis asked if he could sit next to me. Sure, but the hot girls are sitting over there, I thought.

Meanwhile, my head was exploding in pain. The Adonis headed to the bar, returning with a Tooheys New Red, a cup of ice and a towel for my head. I'm in heaven... what movie?

I was unable to watch the movie as I was frozen completely, with the Adonis holding my leg, making sure I was all right. In my head, I planned my entire future with this hot specimen and made up my own movie. In reality, he was gorgeously concerned about me as he tried to snap me back to earth as the actual movie finished. He walked me back to my tent and asked if I would be ok. I said yes, and he was an absolute gentleman, wishing me a good night and saying he'd see me in the morning.

The next day, there was a sea of flurry as it was New Year's Eve. Our friend's boyfriend told us we would be rocking it at the beach that night beside the car park to witness the fireworks. How exciting! Or was it? I hadn't eaten all day as I hadn't seen the Adonis. He was usually with the group of guys we were hanging out with, but today he was missing.

That night, as we descended on the car park with the rest of the tent-goers, we formed a close-knit circle and handed out a few alcoholic beverages. I was feeling sorry for myself as I was sure that the Adonis had either found someone else or had gone home. Trying to open my Tooheys New Red was proving difficult as I'd never drunk beer before.

Suddenly, the Adonis came to my rescue, sat down next to me and asked me if I'd like him to open my beer. I accepted his offer. Even the way he opened the beer can... I couldn't breathe.

With the fireworks countdown on, the Adonis grabbed my hand and led me toward the beach. We stood on the top of the sand dunes, I could hear the waves crashing, and the sound of the first fireworks took off and lit up the sky. The Adonis put his arms around me, and we stood there together. His aftershave melted me completely, his soft breath against my ear.

Pop, pop, pop went the magical fireworks as the Adonis manoeuvred his lips perfectly onto mine. And then there were major fireworks.

Beside myself with excitement, the Adonis suggested we find a dune to lay in while we watch the fireworks and have some of our own fireworks. I couldn't have thought of a more brilliant idea myself. But as we walked down into the dunes, the sand became uneven and thick to walk on. I'm not sure if it was my dazed and confusedness or the fact I'd been sipping on beer for most of the night, but at this particular moment, I lost my footing and the Adonis' hand - and down I went.

Having my rain jacket tied around my waist didn't help because it acted like a slide to my slippery dip. As I hurtled down the dune, I hit something harsh and twisted and very painful. By the time the Adonis and a few others had found me, I was smothered in blood, sand and barbed wire... ouch! It was an old war fence.

As they untangled me from the wreck, I was in a world of hurt. Even the look on Adonis' face indicated how bad my wounds were. My date was completely ruined. An ambulance crew helped me back up the sand dune, and I tried to encourage Adonis to find our friends and hang out with them for the rest of the night since I was going to be patched up at the hospital, then I only wanted my tent and bed. The Adonis tried his best to be supportive, but by now, it was New Year's Day, and the last thing anyone would want was to hang out with a sandy, bloodied mess.

It was almost the last I saw of the Adonis. Off he went to celebrate the new year. As I lay on the mat in my tent, I drifted off, reliving the horror of losing my footing and the Adonis trying to grab my hand but too late.

The following morning, I staggered into the showers, only to witness the full extent of my injuries. No wonder the Adonis left me. I had cuts all over my face, neck and arms – I looked like I'd been in a fight with a chainsaw. Walking back to my campsite, I spotted the Adonis in the distance. He was cuddled up to another girl, one who hadn't had a fight with a chainsaw. Half her luck.

I packed up my tent and waited for my parents to come and collect me.

Chapter 8

Just Do It

Penny Curtis
To: Stephanie Thompson
Re: Swoosh

Lucky my guts told me something wasn't quite right here

Stephanie Thompson
To: Penny Curtis
Re: Swoosh

But you were young, how could you have known?

Penny Curtis
To: Stephanie Thompson
Re: Swoosh

When you know, you know.

During my university years, I had a casual weekend job at Nike, which I loved. I loved what Nike represented. It gave me hope that I, too, could just about do anything if I *Just Did It*. I felt this was conveyed across the business, so all the other employees must feel it, too. There was a positive vibe during work, and the customers thrived off it.

A few months in, one of the guys there and I seemed to hit it off. He was full-time and worked during the week, but he just loved Nike so much he'd come in on weekends to hang out with us. We got talking, and eventually, he asked me out on a date.

We met after one of my work shifts and decided to go ten-pin bowling. It sounded fun. When we met, I noticed he had on the latest Nike sneakers that hadn't even been released yet, and the new Nike terry-towelling tracksuit, also not yet released.

'Wow, how did you score all of that?' I asked, surprised. He ignored me and started organising the bowling balls, which I thought was a little odd.

At Nike, a few months before a product was released, we'd receive a heap of samples. There would be a big staff event whereby we could purchase the Nike samples for next to nothing. Women's sneakers were always a size 6 – my shoe size, so lucky for me, I barely had to pay for sneakers for a long time. Men's sneakers were always a size 9. Apparel was also a specific size.

But this guy was definitely not a size 9 shoe, nor was he the sample apparel size, so I wasn't entirely sure how he could have the sneakers and tracksuit before they went on sale. They should have been packaged up on crates out the back in logistics where no one could touch them. But then I won at bowling which distracted me from thinking about it. Until we caught up again.

He arrived in another new pair of Nike sneakers and apparel not yet released. I was becoming more suspect, but I thought maybe there was a new rule for full-timers. Still, something wasn't sitting right with me, and after our second outing, I decided to call it quits.

Two weeks later, we received an 'All Staff' email indicating that he and two others had been asked to leave and if anyone had information about stolen goods to contact management immediately.

Crikey, sounds like they took Nike's slogan a little too far. "Just take it."

Chapter 9

Get Used To This

Penny Curtis
To: Stephanie Thompson
Re: A little respect

Sometimes on paper they stack up but in reality I'm like 'what was I thinking'.

Stephanie Thompson
To: Penny Curtis
Re: A little respect

Don't beat yourself up, you were trying to be your usual gorgeous self, always thinking of everyone else

Penny Curtis
To: Stephanie Thompson
Re: A little respect

I know but look where it gets me!

My friend and I caught up at our usual after-work Friday bar for a few drinks. Depending on the mood we were in and the talent in the bar, we'd either stay for a big night or leave after a few. Tonight, we were on the fence. But we'd both had an okay week at work, and the talent in the bar was okay, so we decided to stay for one more.

After our fourth 'one more', I was headed to the bathroom when a reasonably attractive guy turned around and asked if he could buy my girlfriend and me a drink. Sure, what's the harm, I thought. He seemed nice enough. Two Hendricks and tonics, please, hold the cucumber in one.

When I got back to the table, Drinks Buyer was already there, ready for conversation. Even though my friend was rolling her eyes behind his back, she was always grateful for the drinks we didn't have to pay for. So, we entertained ourselves with our new drinks were empty, then we both decided it was time to exit stage right. Unfortunately, Drinks Buyers seemed to think he'd been ripped off, so when he asked me for my number, I gave it to him.

I hadn't even got into the taxi when my phone beeped.

I waited until I had got home, brushed my teeth and was in my PJs ready to hop into bed before I put Drinks Buyer at ease and replied back with a message that was vague.

I liked my job. I had a routine that I liked. I liked a late lunch, and I liked my little sandwich shop that was within walking distance who knew exactly how I liked my salad sandwich made. Sometimes, even I was shocked at how good they made my sandwich.

So, it would take a very special someone to come in and be invited to my lunch and my sandwich.

Drinks Buyer thought he was that guy.

At first, he asked me out for dinner. Amateur. First date: low key, maybe a coffee.

He negotiated lunch. Ouch, it might jeopardise my sandwich I loved so much.

But I decided to give him a chance because he was persistent – a sales guy, I suspected.

Lunch, I agreed, at 1:30pm and I only have max 40 minutes, I told him. He seemed confident and said he was counting down the days. Ok, that was kinda sweet but not on my wavelength, so I didn't respond.

The morning of the lunch date and I sent a text to confirm he was still okay for 1:30pm.

He texted back. "Of course, I hope you have a kiss ready for me?"

Why, why do men have to do this? Read the audience, you idiot I don't find any of that romantic or a turn on....I want to run the other way!

I'll admit, I'd made a little more effort in my appearance, but not so much the entire office would start questioning me. It was a juggling act, and they were all nosey. When it was time, I set off for my lunchbreak with exactly enough time to get down to my favourite cafe and be ready for our date.

At exactly 1:30pm I was at our table. I eyed off people ordering the salad that usually went into my sandwich, watching the ingredients slowly go down.

Hurry up Drinks Buyer or I won't be able to get my sandwich.

The clock ticked over to 1:45pm and the waitress asked me if I'd like a drink – they serve alcohol. Yes! I ordered a glass of champagne. My bubbles arrived, but my date still had not.

Panic set in. I really wanted my sandwich, and by now Drinks Buyer was half an hour late with no text update, so I ordered. The sandwich arrived, packaged up to take away, just as Drinks Buyer waltzes in looking smarmy with an expression saying, 'look at me baby I'm so cool you can't but help want me'. He sat down – and went in for the kiss.

I turned my head, and he ate a mouthful of my hair.

He started saying how important he was, and that I should be lucky he showed up at all, and by the way, did I like his suit? As if that wasn't enough, he had the audacity (he has no fucking idea how to read a room) he leaned in and said, "get used to this baby, I'm always late."

Staring at him in bewilderment, I skolled the last of my champagne, bundled up my sandwich and stood up. He is looking dumbfounded. I leaned in, smile slightly and told him, "Get used to this, don't contact me ever again." And with that I walked out the door.

Drinks Buyer must've been still sitting at the cafe table by himself in shock because the next minute I received a text.

"Great performance baby, c'mon back, daddy's waiting."

That made me walk faster back to work, thinking of the precious time I've wasted on not eating my salad sandwich and that some of the salad parts were now making the bread soggy. I started running back to the office to eat my sandwich before it was too late.

Drinks Buyer sent text messages, with no apology for being late. I ignore his texts. But he still doesn't get it. The texts continue.

When I told the story to friend, she agreed that we should avoid our Friday night's drinking bar and try a new one.

A few months later, however, she informs me that Drinks Buyer had pitched a product to her company. His product wasn't good on quality or price, but as she was the decision maker, she told me she was going to teach him a lesson. Apparently, his sales had slumped, and he was desperate for their business. So, the meeting was set.

Drinks Buyer not only turned up to the meeting on time, he arrived early. My friend's receptionist seated him in the waiting area. Where he waited. And waited. At one point he asked the receptionist if everything was OK, and if it wasn't a good time, perhaps they'd like to reschedule.

'No, no, no,' said the receptionist, "it won't be too much longer."

Forty minutes later my friend buzzed the receptionist to show Drinks Buyer into the meeting room. He was sweating bullets as he began spruiking his showmanship routine. My friend sat poised and uninterested in the sales spiel. When he finished, he sat down.

That's when my girlfriend stood up and leaned over to him.

"You don't remember me… but the next time you think it's okay to turn up to meet someone and you're over forty minutes later… well, you can get used to *this*… there's the door. I suggest you pack up your shit and leave immediately. We don't need your type in here."

Right then his eyes lit up as he remembered her from the bar. He went white, but fortunately he packed up and ran out the door with his tail between his legs.

Chapter 10

IDENTITY CRISIS

Penny Curtis
To: Stephanie Thompson
Re: Identity Crisis

How about the poor guy I couldn't recognize?

Stephanie Thompson
To: Penny Curtis
Re: Identity Crisis

Oh, for God's sake, no one would have recognized him! Some days I can't even recognize my own boss! Does that make me a bad person?

Penny Curtis
To: Stephanie Thompson
Re: Identity Crisis

That's because you're drunk for most of the day, I'm surprised you recognise yourself some mornings...

Stephanie and I had had a night out on the town and ended up at a seedy nightclub in the city. After more drinks, I plucked up the courage to go out on the dance floor and have a boogie to the music. After a few minutes I sensed that a guy was trying to get my attention and dance with me. I manoeuvred myself around with my bad dance moves to see if he was worth it and shock horror…he wasn't.

Meanwhile, Stephanie had started chatting to some guys at the bar. I kept dancing by myself, but with the creepy guy who looked like an albino who was about to kill me trying to dance with me. I tried to move away. I tried to give Steph the 'help me out here and get on the dance floor now' look. She ignored me, but one of the guys she was talking to was watching, so I gave him the 'help me' eye.

Fortunately, or unfortunately, he got the hint and came smoothly on the dance floor, where he grabbed me and started dancing with me. Creepy guy got a little disturbed and came closer as if to say, 'hey, she's mine'. But my new-found rescue guy gave creepy guy the hint to back off and creepy guy crept off into the crowd. After the music turned into *doof doof*, we left the dance floor and headed to the bar.

Rescue guy introduced himself as Wes and bought me a drink. I wasn't sure if Wes was my cup of tea, but we kept chatting and he seemed nice. Soon, Stephanie came over and gave me the wind up that we were going. I thanked Wes for saving me and in return he asked me for my number, as he'd like to take me out for dinner. Why not, I owed it to him for saving me from the creepy guy.

Later the next week, Wes contacted me to organise a dinner date. On Thursday, he picked me up and apologises as he mentions he would like to go home first to get changed out of his work gear. I didn't have a problem with this, and we headed to his house. He was very gentlemanlike and organised a platter and a glass of wine for me and turns the music on. He has a mezzanine-style apartment so I can still talk to him while he gets changed.

As I am chatting and looking through his bookshelf, Wes appears halfway down his staircase in an outfit that is definitely not suitable for dining.

I looked up, a little dismayed, but he looked quite excitable as he hopped from one foot to the other with his arms out as if to ask me, "C'mon, c'mon who am I?"

I had no idea who he was now, and it was starting to creep me out. He was wearing a basketball team outfit and was starting to act more like the creep at the nightclub.

It's clear Wes thought I was a basketball fan, which I am not, never have been, nor ever will be, and I was hungry therefore I was hangry! I tell him I'm not into playing Celebrity Head right now and would prefer to go to dinner.

But Wes wasn't budging. He said he'd take me for dinner once I guessed he was.

"Surely ya know. I'm famous. Think a sport."

On that note, I talked out his door, slamming it behind me.

Penny Curtis
To: Stephanie Thompson
Re: Identity Crisis

Yep, it was unfortunate, the poor guy just wanted to be recognized but I wasn't the one to help him out I'm afraid – I've never watched a game of basketball in my life!

Stephanie Thompson
To: Penny Curtis
Re: Identity Crisis

Well, that's not your problem, he needed to carry out more research on his target audience for future reference.

CHAPTER 11

NEVER MIX A MAGPIE WITH A COCKATOO

Penny Curtis
To: Stephanie Thompson
Re: Bet against birds

Seriously, I think I have narrowed it down to the incident after the AFL Grand final

Stephanie Thompson
To: Penny Curtis
Re: Bet against birds

Are you still thinking about this? I think you're being too hard on yourself and over thinking things.

Penny Curtis
To: Stephanie Thompson
Re: Bet against birds

Possibly, but I think if I tick them all off my list, knowing it wasn't entirely my fault, I'll have a clearer path to finding my Mr Right?

Stephanie Thompson
To: Penny Curtis
Re: Bet against birds

If that works for you knock yourself out. Listen, I made a few blunders before I met Graham, and now we're happily married. I didn't go out of my way to beat myself up about all my ex-boyfriends! And nor should you!

Penny Curtis
To: Stephanie Thompson
Re: Bet against birds

You only had two boyfriends before Graham!

Stephanie Thompson
To: Penny Curtis
Re: Bet against birds

Well, you've had some pretty horrendous incidents and it's not far off until you find your Mr. Right. Remind me again of the AFL guy?

September, footy fever, and the city was going nuts. The Collingwood magpies had (tragically) made it into the final against North Melbourne. Neither were my team. A girlfriend usually held our annual football luncheon at her house, but it had become bigger than her house, so this particular year we all agree it made sense to book a table for lunch at a place called The Bot in South Yarra.

With no expense spared, and we all enjoyed a long lunch with matching wines. There were a few familiar faces, and it was nice to catch up while trying to support a team that I didn't barrack for. After Collingwood took victory and our lunch was over, we continued to enjoy a few beverages and our group started to merge with other patrons at the bar.

A friend and I were chatting to a couple of blokes who seemed lovely – however they barracked for Collingwood, not so lovely. At this point I didn't hold this against them. One of them, who I called Roger, started to look a little interesting. He didn't seem too concerned that I may not have had his name correct because the bar was very busy and noisy by now and Roger is excited his team won.

Roger asked me if I was interested in a glass of wine back at his place. He seemed nice enough, but wine only, Roger. We walked back to his apartment, which was massive, and he poured me a glass of wine. The conversation was flowing, but it was all about Collingwood, and not long after I am thinking I need to call a taxi.

But when I looked around, Roger had disappeared. I stood up from the cough and wandered across the living room to his bookshelf to see what he has on display. Suddenly there was noise and a little commotion in the background. I turned to see a naked Roger with a white cockatoo on his arm.

I screamed, dropped my glass, it shattered, the cocky squawked at me and all I could see was Roger's shrivelled appendage and squawking cockatoo! Roger was alarmed, the cockatoo flew off his shoulder and flapped into the walls, then into the bookshelf, and then kamikaze style into the lamp. Feathers were flying everywhere.

"What are you thinking?" I screamed, ducking as the cockatoo swooshed past me and crashed into the bookshelf again, throwing more feathers into the air.

"I thought you'd be turned on by both my cockatoo and my—," Roger screamed back at me.

Swoosh! His cockatoo flew into the window and seemed to pause as it slid down the windowpane. I screamed.

"Just because your AFL team won doesn't mean you have the right to go as cuckoo as your team with your bird naked!" and I ran to collect my belongings and headed out the front door.

Halfway out the building I could still hear the commotion behind me.

Penny Curtis
To: Stephanie Thompson
Re: Bet against birds

Well, that's definitely one AFL game I will remember and not for the sport!

Stephanie Thompson
To: Penny Curtis
Re: Bet against birds

Unfortunately, that's what you can expect from those typical Magpie fans…

CHAPTER 12

WRONG GUY

Penny Curtis
To: Stephanie Thompson
Re: Which one?

It's official, Chinese whispers can mess up lives

Stephanie Thompson
To: Penny Curtis
Re: Which one?

Oh no, what do you mean?

Penny Curtis
To: Stephanie Thompson
Re: Which one?

My girlfriend meant well, but it didn't go according to plan.

One Saturday night, I popped into a local pub to visit a few friends who were all in relationships. I'd just finished work and thought I'd swing past and have a drink with them before I went home. Always great to catch up with the crew, they were good fun people. When I arrived, they'd been there awhile, I could tell by their slightly slurred vocabulary.

After lots of laughs and catching up on all the gossip, it turned to the inevitable question: "Why are you still single?"

I told them all I was fine and that I was very happy. Not convinced by my answer, they took it upon themselves to find me the love of my life at the current location. As one poor unsuspecting guy walked past, they jumped at me and asked me if I liked him. I'm not sure he's my type, I said.

Then another random guy walks past. "How about him?" My friends are yelling now, like it's a gameshow.

"Nope, not me."

It went on, and it was entertaining but I wasn't interested.

Finally, I ordered some drinks at the bar and began talking to a lovely guy who was a landscape architect. His name was Tom, he was charming, and we hit it off. Tom introduced me to his mate Kyle, an engineer, and we exchanged polite small talk. Then I left to dish out the drinks to my friends.

I excused myself to go to the bathroom and on my return, Tom and Kyle called my name. I stopped and talked a little more with them. Tom was lovely. Definitely my type.

On my return to my friends, rumour has already got back to the group that I've been flirting with these guys. Soon I was being drilled on who they were, what they did. Seriously, it was like a circus but with the best intentions.

It was getting late and I had an early start in the morning. My friend asked me to point out the guy I liked so I point out the landscaper, then left, thinking nothing more of it.

When I woke up the next morning early for work, I checked my phone to see a trail of text messages from my friends from the previous night. It seems my girlfriend had gone up to the landscaper and given him my number.

One of the text messages was from Tom, the landscape gardener or so I thought. How embarrassing, but respectfully he was polite enough to find it quite funny. Phew.

"0418 507 506"

Hi there, we met the other night, your friend said you thought I was ok. I thought you were too. How about a drink? ☺

When I return from work that afternoon, I respond to my girlfriend who is beside herself for setting me up with this guy and wants to hear all the details of our first date. I then pluck up the courage to respond to "Tom" and we eventually organise to catch-up the following Saturday afternoon.

Throughout the week there's some text messaging with "Tom" and myself. I make a few comments about the weather and working outdoors, and his replies seem normal.

On the Saturday, I'm a little early to the bar and look around, no one I know thank god. I organise myself a drink and sit myself down at a table. My nerves are building. I send Tom a text just to let him know I'm here. He responds back indicating that he's already here and has a drink waiting for me. Shocked, I look around. Towards the back of this dimely lit bar I see a bloke sitting by himself with an extra drink.

As I walk towards him, I realise that this isn't Tom the landscape gardener but Tom's mate the engineer, Kyle. Unfortunately, that look of disappointment must have been all over my face, because the poor guy says, "I'm not who you were expecting am I?"

So, I reply "I'll be honest, you're not, I liked your mate the landscape gardener – sorry."

No feelings lost whatsoever, and we stayed and had a drink together.

Turns out my girlfriend had gone up to them both and told them that I liked Kyle the engineer, and Tom the landscaper was a little annoyed. However, turns out Tom the landscaper was in a relationship already and as Kyle mentioned he would have broken my heart. Poor Kyle did try to convince me to go out with him again, but he wasn't my type.

Chapter 13

Pearl Earrings

Penny Curtis
To: Stephanie Thompson
Re: Pearl earring

I thought this was where sport meets love

Stephanie Thompson
To: Penny Curtis
Re: Pearl earring

Well, it sort of was but only for a fleeting moment

Penny Curtis
To: Stephanie Thompson
Re: Pearl earring

Fleeting and a significant loss

Our triathlon had some pretty wild end-of-season parties. For the majority of the year, we were in training mode and there was barely any alcohol drunk. So come end of season, and even the smell of alcohol could set us off.

Great people, fit bodies. Everyone supported each other. A team effort, regardless of your abilities. There was one male body that caught my attention this particular season. I'd seen him a few times throughout the years, but he'd come back and was looking sharp. He was a little more athletic than me. He swam in the fast lane, he was in the early group for cycling, and when it came to running, he just ran straight past me.

Look, we can all dream. So, that season I dreamt that he and I became a couple and let's just say it nearly eventuated. My poor girlfriend had to put up with my crazy tactics.

We'd have a mid-season party which was quite tame, and he showed up. He was very aloof. I tried a few dance moves, but he was too focused on his training ride for the next day. Boring. So, the next day while I was recovering from a hangover, he swam, cycled and ran for half the morning.

As the season came to a close, on the odd occasion he did notice me, and we had a chat in some of our training sessions. I was beside myself and could barely talk.

The end of season Christmas party arrived, and everyone was very excited to celebrate all our hard training throughout the year. Everyone was frocked up and ready to party. Corks were popping and canopies were flowing. I spot the athlete I was totally head-over-heels with. My girlfriend reminded me it was a long night and to keep it together. Always great advice.

When the DJ started up, we all hit the dance floor. Great music, great dance moves, and terrible singing, especially to the chorus. Everyone was having the best time. More alcohol was consumed. The dance moves got sillier. The next minute we've all formed a circle. Our club president is in the middle with half his shirt off and my girlfriend is taking it upon herself to undo the rest of it.

Men's ties began flying around the room, and as I shook my booty, I realised hot spunk of a triathlete was dancing right next to me. I pretended I haven't noticed him and kept dancing. The scene stepped up another notch and more clothes were flying off. Some amazing dance moves came from the athletes you would think were the most conservative people in the world.

I went for a quick bathroom stop, and clearly the alcohol was impacting some of us more than others. There were a few girls holding the hair back over the porcelain. I escaped the mess and headed back out. Clearly someone with sense had put away a few of the bottles of unopened alcohol and refreshed with water. And someone else had told the DJ to calm the tunes down so we were onto love songs and dedications.

So, we were all dancing very closely together on the dance floor and as I turned around, I was spun into the arms of the hot athletic guy I'd been dreaming about all season. He was tall, dark and way too handsome for his own good. We were dancing close. He has his hands all over me. He pulled me closer. *I am in heaven.* Then closer again, and this time our lips nearly touch. It was getting heated. He had all the moves, and I was a rag doll but enjoying every second.

The DJ announced the last song for the night, a slow, romantic 'get in close with your partner,' song. Hot athletic guy started gliding me around the dance floor. I'm in awe. He slowed us down, my heart was pounding. Please kiss me, I think.

He started nibbling my neck, which was a great start. He moved up to my hear and began sucking on it, which was okay for a moment, then I felt something odd, but I ignored it because I was too excited for what was coming next. The music hit a high and he swapped sides and nibbled the other side of my neck then sucks on my ear. A little gross but he's so hot, I can ignore it.

He pushed me back, holding my hands. That's when I notice, through the strobe lights, he has my earrings – both my earrings – in his teeth and is smiling back at me. I wasn't sure how I was meant to react. From behind, he gets bumped by a terrible dance move from behind, then he and I look at each other in exclamation as we realised: he'd just swallowed my pear earrings!

He thought it was funny. I wasn't so sure, thinking of how I'm meant to get them back… after he's gone to the toilet? My friend staggers overlooking green and says it's time to go home. Hot athlete, now with my earrings inside his belly, grabbed a pen and wrote his number on my hand, kisses it, and tells me to call him.

Our next training session was light, a cruisy 40-kilometre bike ride before Saturday morning brunch. Many stories were coming out from the Christmas party. Some very funny ones, some not so funny. Then they started asking me what was going on with hot athlete. I told them the story about the earrings, then explained they were sentimental, and that I've tried calling him a few times but haven't heard back.

One of the guys in the bike pack cycles next to me. "You know he's married with a kid, don't you?" I nearly fell off my bike. I was even more unimpressed as he had probably passed my earrings out his rear end by now. I decided Hot Athlete deserved to be with his wife and kid. I could save up for another pair of pearl earrings.

Chapter 14

Coaster-man

Penny Curtis
To: Stephanie Thompson
Re: Formula One

If only you could predict, or look into a glass ball and see the disaster that's waiting for you

Stephanie Thompson
To: Penny Curtis
Re: Formula One

Well then it wouldn't be called life, would it?

I was working at my regular part-time gig at a local pub opposite the Australian Grand Prix track. It was the Formula One weekend, and we were excited because we'd finally have people to serve. The shift usually went painfully slowly even if we had a few drinks ourselves whilst our manager wasn't watching.

I had been fortunate enough to secure the afternoon into evening shifts for Thursdays to Mondays. Cashing! I loved it as I needed as many shifts as possible because I was saving to buy a property. After finishing university, I'd race down to the pub and start my shift.

So many people were interested in Formula One. I didn't mind it, more for the skill level than anything else. On Thursday afternoon, the qualifying rounds had nearly finished, and petrol heads had made their way into the pub, which was starting to spill out onto the side road. It was manic but a great atmosphere.

Two nice-looking, slightly older guys were perched on stools in the corner of the bar, observing everyone and making funny comments. I served them throughout the afternoon and late into the night. They were very good at tipping, so I slipped them a free drink every now and then.

I particularly liked one, and he seemed interested in me. At the end of the night when he was well and truly at his quota and about to leave, he slipped me a $20 tip on top of a coaster with a picture drawn on it.

It was a male and female stick figure on an island, and underneath he'd written:

Let's make this dream a reality.

He winked and said, "see you same place, same time tomorrow". I took the twenty and the coaster and stuffed them into my back pocket.

On Friday night, as the qualifiers were winding down, the pub was already starting to overflow with people, and I was busy serving drinks to thirsty Formula One fans. Suddenly, Mr Coaster-man and his mate were sitting perched up on the bar stools, same place as yesterday. Throughout the night I made sure to look after them and slipped them a few free drinks again. I tried to encourage them to visit other great local Melbourne bars, but they were adamant that this was their favourite. Mr Coaster-man and I hit it off again, he had me in hysterics most of the night. And once again at the end of the night he slipped me a twenty and another coaster with another stick-figure drawing on the back.

On Saturday, I had an all-day shift, which finished late as someone had called in sick so, basically, I had scored a double shift which technically was a triple shift, since I didn't finish until midnight. Our large TVs were showing the races live, which encouraged people who couldn't get tickets to the Formula One to come in earlier to watch. The atmosphere was buzzing.

When a couple of blokes came towards the bar and were about to perch on the two seats my mates normally sat, I told them those seats were taken, even though I had no idea if those two jokers would return.

Whilst busy serving someone, I heard suddenly Mr. Coaster-man's voice shout out, "How does anyone get any decent service around here?"

A colleague of mine jumped in to serve them. But perched on the edge of their usual seats, Mr Coaster-man exclaimed he wasn't happy being served by someone else and in future he'd prefer it if I served them. Seriously, that audacity of this bloke! But he had a devilish smile that I couldn't resist.

Soon the bar was packed and ten-deep of people waiting for a drink. There were so many staff behind the bar we could hardly move.

I served one guy who barely came up to the bar, even with his spikes in his hair. He was flanked by two huge security guys that no one could push or shove because they were that big. They wore dark glasses, which I thought was funny because the bar was dimly lit.

"Pint of Guinness, love," the short guy shouted out.

I hate pouring Guinness – it took forever, which meant less tips.

"Is that all?" I asked as I handed it to him.

He smiled but didn't say a word. Weirdo. He took his Guinness and handed me over a one hundred dollar note, and says "keep the change, love".

What?! Are you kidding me, I just made a ninety-buck tip.

I resolved to pour more Guinness in future.

My two clowns at the corner of the bar were yelling at me to come and serve them. I finally got across to them with their beers.

"Do you know who that was?" Mr. Coaster-man asked me.

"Absolutely no idea, but he needs to get his security mates to lift him up in future so he can see over the bar, the poor guy!"

My two bar friends were in hysterics. "You just served Rod Stewart a Guinness!"

I couldn't believe it. "What? Are you two having me on?"

From nowhere my manager came past and said, "you could have poured Rod a Guinness and NOT charged him for it!"

Whoops….

As the evening came to a close, I felt exhausted, but Mr Coaster-man and his friend wanted to know where they should go next. They decided on the casino, which I encouraged, and they invited me.

Just for an hour or two, I thought, as I had to work all day Sunday. Before we left, I reminded Mr Coaster-man that he had forgotten to draw the next coaster. He obliged.

Sure, it probably wasn't my best move agreeing to chaperone these two clowns at the Casino, they were like two little kids in a lolly shop. We ended up at a blackjack table.

I've never played Blackjack before, nor was I about to start. But these two pulled out wads of cash, and they were off! Half drunk, spending all their cash, they won one then lost a whole lot more. It was early morning by now, and somehow, I ended up with another drink in my hand. Mr Coaster-man's friend decided to have a go at a different game and left us to our drinks.

Mr Coaster-man started talking. The more he spoke, the more he drivelled. *I'd had enough, I'm out*. I went to leave and then Mr Coaster-man asked if we could spend the night together, no sex just cuddling. I told him I'd like that but unfortunately, I had to work in five hours and needed some sleep. He said he understood and was entertaining enough to draw a wayward coaster.

I honestly didn't expect to see them again, yet as Sunday's event came to a close with the live music we could hear in the pub, they walked in. It was like our last hoorah together, so I made sure they were looked after. Throughout the evening they provided much entertainment. I was beginning to fancy Mr Coaster-man and I felt he was feeling the same. At one point when he excused himself, his mate called me over and told me Mr Coaster-man really liked me and was wanting to give me his number to see if we could continue our friendship. I had nothing to lose although I wasn't sure if I was any good at a long-distance relationship.

Mr Coaster-man and I swapped numbers.

When I finished my shift, they tried to encourage me to go out with them, I had my full-time job on Monday and was shattered. As Mr Coaster-man handed me over my last coaster he gave me a lingering kiss which was exactly what I needed. I took his twenty-dollar tip, my coaster and his phone number and walked away.

Many text messages and phone calls later, I felt I'd finally met my match. He was talking about heading back for a weekend in Melbourne soon. Then something interesting happened.

I got a text message from his wife.

Yes, that's right, his wife.

It wasn't a nice text message – she basically threatened me. "If you ever go anywhere near my husband or call or text him again, I will track you down myself and I will hurt you."

Hmm…not the type of text you really want to receive. I text back and indicated that she needed to hurt her lying husband instead. I blocked his number.

Over the next few weeks, I had a few private numbers call on my phone, and then randomly, he somehow worked out my email address. He was a typical, sad lying bloke with pity a story, not an apology, on how unloved he is in his loveless relationship and was miserable.

I didn't come to the pity party though, oh no.

I left him to his own pity party while I gathered up all the coasters he had given me, and set them on fire.

Chapter 15

Driza-Bone

Penny Curtis
To: Stephanie Thompson
Re: Driza-Bone

I always liked an outback farmer – but urban farmers not so much.

Stephanie Thompson
To: Penny Curtis
Re: Driza-Bone

Was he a farmer?

Penny Curtis
To: Stephanie Thompson
Re: Driza-Bone

I don't think so, but he's now ruined any farmer that I ever meet who wears a Driza-Bone coat.

We knew a couple of the regular guys at the popular local pub. If either Steph or I were running late, these guys would keep the other one company until the other one arrived. They were harmless, and lovely guys. Both were into AFL and at times we'd watch a game on the big screen and have a few drinks with them, all harmless fun.

On one occasion Steph was running late and only one of the guys was there, he bought me a glass of champagne and we politely talked about life. His kids were a little older now and nearing finishing school, he also dropped in that his wife and he were thinking about getting divorced. "You know, we just stayed together for the kids' sake." Sad, but that's where he was at.

Thankfully Steph showed up, apologising for being late, it was pouring with rain and apparently her tram had hit a pedestrian. Our male friend bought us both a round of drinks and half an hour later his mate finally made an appearance. As the night wore on Steph and the other mate were having a debate about something. So, the first mate decided he'd had enough drinks under his belt to ask me out to next weekend's AFL, and how about a kiss to seal the deal. Gross for the kiss but okay for the members tickets to the semi-final AFL.

I received a few text messages throughout the week from my AFL date, who was more nervous than I was about where to meet and what to wear, as if I'd never been to the members' before. On the afternoon of the game, I met him at the required gate, where he complimented me on my dress choice and decided that also deserved a kiss – but this time with tongue. Gross again. I wasn't remotely interested in him. But I was interested in watching my team get through to the finals, so I guess I took one for the team so to speak. I'm not sure who dressed him, but he had the wrong dress code – he looked like he was dressed for the polo. He had on an Akubra hat (didn't suit him), moleskins (which were far too tight), a pink shirt (which would be okay for the polo but neither AFL teams' colours were pink) and this smelly Driza-Bone coat that went all the way to his R.M Williams boots – which he could have cleaned.

Hopefully they'd let me into the members area, but I wasn't confident for my friend with the tickets.

Unfortunately, we both made it through, and were shown to our table for one of those fancy luncheons with a key guest speaker.

Sitting at the table next him, this bloke went to introduce himself and asked, "And this is the new girlfriend you've been telling us about?"

I nearly spat my champagne out and correctly stated that I was, "just a friend, not a girlfriend," which my date seemed upset by. My eyes were darting around the room for the waiter to re-fill my empty champagne glass. By the end of the lunch, I had corrected every bloke at the table that I was merely a friend.

They made an announcement that the game was about to start, and taking my glass of champagne along, we found our seats. But I noticed my friend was acting a little strange. I wasn't sure how much he'd had to drink because throughout lunch I was just looking after myself to ensure my glass was always topped up with the lovely French bubbles.

Beside me I could see him keep looking over his shoulder. Just as the game started, he moved seats so there was a gap between us – of three seats. His excuse… "I can get a bit vocal, best you don't know who I am during the game," he said as he laughed at his own stupidity. In my mind, I was thinking just give me the tickets and I'd probably enjoy myself more without your unusual actions.

First quarter: my team was winning, and my champagne glass was full. I'm not sure if my date saw the first quarter, he was too busy in disguise and pretending to be on his phone the entire game. Very odd behaviour.

At the start of the second quarter, he jumped up and walked backwards, asking me if I'd like another drink. *Yes, of course, thank you.* But as the second quarter was nearing its end, I realised I felt a little parched and was wondered where my friend had got too. It was odd. As the little kids came onto the field for the half-time entertainment, Glen, who had been sitting at our table came up to me with the glass of champagne and smiled at me.

"For the lady."

"Thanks," I responded. As I took a sip, Glen asked if the seat next to me was taken.

"Please, it's all yours. Clearly my friend isn't interested in sitting next to me."

As the siren sounded for the third quarter, Glen explained to me that my friend was in a little spot of bother. He'd run into his wife who was here with her father. Apparently, she had the members tickets, not him. They had had a run-in upstairs when he went to buy the drinks, and Blake had left abruptly.

Well, that explained his behaviour during the first quarter – he must have spotted them. Yes, he definitely knew how to impress a lady.

Well, at least Glen was nice enough to ensure my champagne was always full, and even better, my team won and were into the final.

Pity Blake left, though, I would have kissed him again to get tickets off him for the final.

The next time I met Steph at our local for a drink, Blake wasn't anywhere to be seen. But his mate Jack turned up. He'd heard about the incident and was very apologetic. I told him he was just lucky that my team had won.

Chapter 16

BEACHED WHALE

Penny Curtis
To: Stephanie Thompson
Re: Beached Whale

There's something about men and saltwater

Stephanie Thompson
To: Penny Curtis
Re: Beached Whale

Yes, you don't seem to have much luck with the salty ones

After competing in the annual Portsea Swim Classic, a few friends and I decided to have something to eat at the Portsea Hotel. It was a beautiful day, and everyone was in good spirits after the swim, with heaps of people milling around.

We were sitting eating next to a group of guys who were about our age. One of our girlfriends, who hadn't swum and may have had one too many beers and was becoming a little vocal. She was getting annoyed because one of the guys wasn't responding as fast as what she would have liked.

At one point, in her frustration, she leaned in and yelled at him, "Are you deaf?".

It turns out he was.

We jumped up and rescued them both, apologising to the guy for our friend. As the evening went on, I continued the conversation with another guy from the same group. He loved swimming just as much as I did, and we had a lot of other things in common. We worked out we had gone to the same university at the same time but studied different courses.

Around midnight, I had had enough. It had been a big day – an early start driving to Melbourne, the 1.5-kilometre swim followed by a long afternoon. It was time for me to go to bed. The guy encouraged me to stay out longer and have a few more drinks with him, but I was pooped. So, he scribbled his number on my hand and asked if he could see me again when we were next back in Melbourne.

Of course, I'd like to catch up again. He seemed nice.

The next morning, I was up early before my friends and before we had to check out to head back home. I decided to go for a walk along the beach and take in the amazing scenery. I'd been walking for approximately half an hour when I noticed a lump up ahead. I wasn't one hundred percent sure how to describe the lump as it looked a little awkward. I kept walking towards it. Another beach walker and their dog coming towards me also noticed the lump. The walker avoided the lump, but the dog sniffed at it until its owner called it away.

As I neared the lump, I realised it was a human body – a very white male human body. It was wrapping itself around another male body, and both bodies were naked and passed out.

That was too much to see at that hour of the morning. As I walked past a few metres away from these entangled bodies, one of them looked very familiar. It was the guy I had been talking to the previous night who had given me his phone number.

Out of respect for other passers-by, there was some seaweed nearby, so and I placed it over the top of their private parts, so no one had to witness that and made sure they were actually alive. As I walked on past, I made a note next to his phone number 'beached whale' and reminded myself to never take his call. Finishing my walk on the beach I passed two policemen walking down onto the beach pointing at the two lumps passed out on the beach.

Chapter 17

Salty Ol' Sea Dog

Stephanie Thompson
Penny Curtis
Re: That Ol' Sea Dog

We all held our breath for the Sailor though, it was nearly a positive experience.

Penny Curtis
To: Stephanie Thompson
Re: That Ol' Sea Dog

I don't think "nearly positive" really cuts it Steph, I mean let's be serious.

Stephanie Thompson
To: Penny Curtis
Re: That Ol' Sea Dog

No, you're right, he was just a salty old sea dog who took advantage of you and then dumped you in the deep dark waters

A friend and I were out walking along the St Kilda Esplanade when we decided to stop at the marina café for a juice. Minding our business, a bloke came up and started talking to us. He was a smooth talker and wasn't bad to look at either. He asked us if we were interested in sailing.

"Sort of, maybe, thank you, but we're just here trying to enjoy our juice."

He left his number and offered to invite us out on his boat.

A few days later, my friend told me that she texted the guy on my behalf, and that he'd invited me out on his boat this Saturday.

Unbelievable! I mean, seriously, thanks for trying, but I am capable of finding my own dates. Or maybe I'm not?

He texted me, and he was very charming. We went out on his boat with his friends, and they were all really lovely. He definitely knew how to charm the pants of people, so to speak.

We had more boat dates, this time just the two of us, and I was starting to fall for him. Then he dropped a bombshell and casually mentioned that he had to sail to Sydney for business. I wondered why he couldn't fly up instead.

He said he's not sure how long he would be up there, but he might fly me up for a weekend of two. True to his word, he purchased a return ticket for me to meet him in Sydney for a weekend, and knowing I liked theatre, he bought tickets for us to see The Lion King.

I couldn't believe it. I arrived on Saturday morning and taxied to the Cruising Yacht Club where his boat was moored. We spent the morning walking around the area, then he mentioned he's organized lunch on his boat. Then we went sailing. I reminded him that the Lion King started at 7pm, so we needed to be back by 5pm at the latest. He seemed to ignore my suggestion.

We had a lovey day out on the water. He was charming, the sun was shining, and we were enjoying each other's company. As the day progressed, I noticed he was taking us out through the heads. I did a quick calculation – it'd taken us approximately four hours to sail to get to this point as there wasn't much wind.

If it took us another three hours to get back, we'd be rushed for the theatre, we might even miss the show. I mentioned it to him as we sailed through the heads. He filled my glass with more champagne and assured me he had everything in hand.

Clearly not. We sailed back into the marina at around midnight.

Worse, there were never any tickets to The Lion King.

I'm not sure what game he was playing, but Sunday was pretty miserable, so I decided to head early to the airport. His charm was wearing off. When I returned to Melbourne, I made the decision to end it. He was aloof, as if nothing had gone on, and proceeded to tell me of some sailing adventures he was working on to sail around Australia.

A few months later, I received a text from him, indicating after high seas he had made it to Perth. Unbelievable! How about a 'How are you?'. So, I decided to give him nothing back and didn't respond.

At Christmas, he had the audacity to text me again. The first few messages were all about his sailing trip. Then came a message that he'd missed me terribly and was inviting me to a party with some of his friends.

I fell for his charm again.

At the party it was clear he'd told everyone I was his girlfriend. I was confused. It was awkward. He was all over me and I wasn't impressed. He tried to kiss me every moment he could. I refused. He confessed he had made a mistake and asked how he could ever make it up to me. Over a bottle of champagne, I gave in, and confessed I did have feelings for him.

Over the next few weeks, was intense. There was emotion. There were feelings. There was sailing and verve and laughter. He told me he was falling in love with me.

I was on a cloud.

Then another bombshell.

He had decided to do one last sailing trip. He wanted to sail to Europe via the islands which can be dangerous – possibly pirates. He could be killed! He said he'd contact me at various stages of the trip and fly me over to meet him and spend time with him. I'm overwhelmed, but I don't want to lose him.

On his last night in town, it was emotional. The Salty Ol' Sea Dog told me all the right things – it was too good to be true and yet I believed every word he said. It was like a fantasy, imagining him in all these exotic places while he battled the elements. In an emotional farewell, I watched him sail into the sunset as he left Port Philip Bay.

A few days later, worried that he hasn't contacted me as agreed from Eden, I tried contacting him by text and email. When I heard nothing, I imagined the worst.

The following weekend I met my friend for an afternoon walk along St Kilda Esplanade. I shared with her my woes about the Sailor and she listened intently with all her support. After a juice, we walked past the sailing club, and I noticed Salty Old Sea Dog's car parked down the side of a shed. Maybe the club had agreed he could leave his car there as a safe place while he battled seas around the world.

I say goodbye to my friend, and as we drove our separate ways. I decided to do a drive-by his car. To my shock, he was standing right there, talking to someone.

Am I dreaming? I do a U-turn. No, not dreaming – there he was.

I nearly crashed my car. The liar! Anger built up. I pulled over and immediately called Steph. She asked me if I was sure it was him. I was 100% sure.

So, we devised a plan.

Playing the damsel in distress, I sent him another text and email with my concern for his safety. That evening I received a response. He said there had been some bad weather, so he had to turn back, and he was nearing Eden. Reception was really bad, he said.

I bet it is, you ol' dog.

That evening, Steph and I took her car down to the sailing club. We parked in the carpark one over, then crept in the dark up to his car. When I peered inside, I could see a picture of his dead dog on the dashboard. Suddenly there was movement on the sailing club's patio bar, and I was Salty Ol' Sea Dog finishing his beer. He put down his glass and started walking down the stairs to his car.

Steph and I ran for it, then in a panic I dived into the bushes that lined the club's entrance. I wanted, holding my breath, as he got into his car and reversed out straight past me.

I was in shock. I couldn't believe it. Why would someone make up they were sailing around the world? I didn't message him again.

But a few months later, I received another text about his trials and tribulations on the high seas. I ignored it.

Finally, a few years later I was out with another friend when I bumped into the Salty Ol' Sea Dog. He said he was surprised I never responded to any of his messages. I gave him the look of 'Are you kidding me?'. I explained I had seen him in Melbourne when he was meant to be halfway up the eastern seaboard, yet he denied it all. I know what I saw, and I had a witness.

I think the salt had got to him.

Chapter 18

The Mauler

A kiss may ruin a human life.
Oscar Wilde

Penny Curtis
To: Stephanie Thompson
Re: Is this my lowest point?

I was on the bus this morning heading to work and as we were stuck in traffic on the Sydney Harbour Bridge. I looked out and saw that guy we used to run with who took a fancy to me. Gosh he's obviously stopped running, he's the size of a bus!

Stephanie Thompson
To: Penny Curtis
Re: Is this my lowest point?

Might actually be my lowest point….just hurled in the bathroom! Can't recall even running at this point only for the porcelain

Penny Curtis
To: Stephanie Thompson
Re: Is this my lowest point?

Sounds like you've hit a low point at 9:18am – are you pregnant?! Yes, you remember it was just you and I and those guys from your law firm, we'd do a lap of Kirribilli and then back across the bridge

Stephanie Thompson
To: Penny Curtis
Re: Is this my lowest point?

It's a little sketchy but I do recall running with you with some lovely guys. And no, I am not pregnant. If I was it would be a miracle as Graham has had the snip.

Stephanie was an executive assistant at a prestigious law firm, and every Thursday she invited me to join her and some colleagues, including Zac, for a run across the Harbour Bridge and around the north shore. It was something I looked forward to because they were a nice bunch, and although I wasn't as fast as they were, they were always kind enough to include me and wait for me, especially during the winter months.

On the odd occasion, one of them would organise a social gathering which was usually just a drink after the run at a pub at the Rocks – fun, but very lawyer focused. Every now and then there was a suggestion of us all doing a dinner, but nothing seemed to come about.

Zac was a very good runner, so we both felt like we were holding him back as he'd wait for us to show us the route.

On the Friday after the Thursday night run, I was flat out at work and trying to get through my one hundred emails when I noticed one from Zac. How lovely, he was organising a dinner on Saturday night for all of us! I replied promptly with a yes and asked him to let me know what I can bring. As Saturday night approached, I sent Stephanie a text offering to pick her up on the way to Zac's. No response.

Zac answered the door and seemed to be quite dressed up for a casual dinner at his place. I handed him a bottle of wine and asked if I could do anything to help whilst we waited for everyone else. Zac poured us both a glass of champagne and there was a bit of awkward conversation. I realised on reflection that we had hardly ever spoken during the run session (since I could hardly breathe).

I mentioned I had texted Stephanie offering to pick her up on the way through but hadn't heard from her. All I got from Zac was an 'Oh yeah right' as he continued to cut the pumpkin skin off with a sharp knife towards his wrists.

I looked around the kitchen and out to the small dining area where I noticed the table is set – for two!

Christ! Where's the other place settings?

I skolled my champagne in a panic. Zac poured me another glass and asked if I like pumpkin risotto.

"Love it!" I exclaimed, desperately trying to cover up my alarm. As Zac put the lid on the risotto, he suggested we move to his couch to relax and talk further.

Sitting as far into one end as I possibly could on the two-seater, Zac plonked himself right next to me, and moved his hand to my knee. Now, we ran together, but I didn't think I had ever given Zac the sign that I was interested. Except, maybe, accidentally accepting his invitation to a dinner for two?

From out of nowhere, Zac launched at me. Perhaps he was trying to enact a kiss he'd seen from a movie, but all I got was a mauling similar to an excitable puppy that licks you all over your face. And it didn't seem to end – Zac was very committed.

Trying to not look like I was mortified, but also to not encourage another mauling, I pulled back just as the timer went off in the kitchen. Zac jumped up to stir the risotto.

"Hungry?" Zac called from the kitchen. I'm not sure I had an appetite anymore, but it would have been impolite to run out the front door.

I excused myself quickly to find tissues and wipe off the saliva that's all over my face. I send Stephanie a quick text – Thanks for your no show! – and head back to the dining table with the setting for two.

We sit at the table, and I try my best not to show any sarcasm as I exclaim, "Oh it's only us for dinner, I see".

Zac looked confused but tucked into his pumpkin risotto.

The rice was crunchy, but I've got to be more flexible, I told myself. Actually no, I don't I've just been mauled! Thank goodness for the wine.

Zac cleared the plates and suggested we relax on the couch – I panicked, making up the excuse that I had a really early start in the morning. Zac asked if it was a fun run, and I indicated it was personal. I told him I had a really good time (a complete lie) and that I looked forward to seeing him for a run on Thursday.

Zac went in for another mauling and said he'd see me before then.

What a disaster, I thought. I'm going to have to find a new running club…

Stephanie Thompson
To: Penny Curtis
Re: Is this my lowest point?

It was partly your fault, you should have studied the email more carefully, as no one else was copied on the email. Zac was inviting just you.

Penny Curtis
To: Stephanie Thompson
Re: Is this my lowest point?

I agree, but I didn't deserve the mauling!

Stephanie Thompson
To: Penny Curtis
Re: Is this my lowest point?

No, you're right you didn't deserve to be mauled so put that one behind you now.

Chapter 19

NOSE DRIPPER

Penny Curtis
To: Stephanie Thompson
Re: Etiquette

When I was going out, my mum always used to ask, "have you got your handkerchief?" What's with today's world, have they run out?

Stephanie Thompson
To: Penny Curtis
Re: Etiquette

Our Mum's are the same, she still asks me. The other day on the tram coming to work, I saw a guy wipe his nose on his sleeve of his lovely suit.

Penny Curtis
To: Stephanie Thompson
Re: Etiquette

Gross! At least he recognised his nose was runny.

We hadn't even started our meal yet and he had a stalactite dangling from his nose. I started sniffing thinking that by osmosis he might sniff himself. The clear clump of snot hanging from his nose was mesmerising, I totally ignored his question to me.

This gave him the indication that I was interested in his conversation but in all seriousness, I was fascinated how he had no knowledge that he had a clump of snot just dangling. He waiter came over and dropped off some menus as we ordered drinks. I think the waiter even glanced twice at this clear clip of gunk just dangling out of his nose.

I've just met this guy. In my mind, I wasn't sure if I liked him, so do I give him any indication that he had snot dangling from his nose? Or would he think I was rude and leave the date, but did I really care? Thank God, the drinks came, so I didn't have to make the decision. Finally, he wiped his nose. OK, let me rephrase that… he wiped his nose – with his sleeve. Oh Jesus, who is this neanderthal?

We ordered our meal, the Thai dishes coming out of the kitchen looked scrumptious. The conversation continued, it was a bit dry, unlike his nose. Whilst waiting for our meal and I was in mid-conversation, another stalactite appeared out of his nose, just hanging in the breeze. Could he not feel this on his bare skin? Was he playing me? Again, my osmosis kicked in and I sniffed, to no avail. I even unfolded my serviette and wiped my nose pretending to blow it, even excusing myself, he didn't get it.

I was still staring at his snot hanging when our meal arrived. We'd ordered a few different dishes to share. The food looked delicious.

Until I watched in slow motion as he served us both one of the first dishes, his dangling snot started to extend. So much so, it left the cave and dripped straight onto my plate. He didn't notice a thing. As he put the serving spoon down, he handed me my plate with a smile and then wiped his nose again with his sleeve.

Dilemma. What do I do? I can't see the clear snot that's now landed on my plate. He's devouring his plate like it's his last supper. Meanwhile, I'm trying to quickly think of how I can get out of eating his snot that's floating somewhere in my meal.

Picking up my water glass, oh low and behold it's a little slippery and, all of a sudden, my water glass has spilt onto my plate just enough to water down my meal enough it is now not edible. Winning. He's looking at me like I'm some klutz, but little does he know I'm avoiding his snot.

Somehow, I manage to serve myself the remaining meals. No snot sightings but the conversation isn't there, and in fairness I am more interested in when the next drip is coming out of his nose. Not a good sign in my eyes for a second date. We pass on dessert and coffee, and I am keen to escape.

Outside the restaurant, he's waiting with me for a taxi and as I turn to look at him, there's yet another snot dangler starring right back at me. And in an unexplainable moment he captures the stalactite in his hands, and looks at it, studies it, laughs and then wipes it on his chest, exclaiming, "Cold night, my nose is running," and laughs.

I was grateful my taxi arrived.

Chapter 20

Stock Market Crash

Penny Curtis
To: Stephanie Thompson
Re: When My Shares Went Down

Oh dear, I feel as if my shares have hit a low point

Stephanie Thompson
To: Penny Curtis
Re: When My Shares Went Down

Since when have you owned any shares?

Penny Curtis
To: Stephanie Thompson
Re: When My Shares Went Down

Well, apparently, I own some in my superannuation from working all my life, but I'm not talking about those!

Stephanie Thompson
To: Penny Curtis
Re: When My Shares Went Down

I see, you're talking about you personally, and you feel your stocks have crashed, and are worth nothing – send in the administrators?!

Penny Curtis
To: Stephanie Thompson
Re: When My Shares Went Down

That's a little drastic, but I didn't have the correct set-up on this occasion and my stocks went plummeting.

Stephanie Thompson
To: Penny Curtis
Re: When My Shares Went Down

Do tell…he looked pretty sexy when I dropped you off for dinner.

He was sexy, in fact, too sexy for his own good. No thanks to my dear boss who was always on the lookout for me.

We were in Perth for a conference and after a successful day we were having pre-dinner drinks. Everything was going well until I heard a sexy voice behind me introduce himself to my boss. My boss then introduced me to Hamish, and I could not speak. I froze completely – because he was just too good looking.

It got worse. My boss, detecting how uncomfortable I was, decided to invite Hamish to join us for a drink, and started the banter, which I was usually quite good at, but on this occasion, I couldn't even string a sentence together and made a complete twat of myself. Hamish and my boss seemed to think it was quite entertaining. I did not. A few drinks later and my boss decided two things:

1. When Hamish was back in Melbourne, he needed to contact me so we could work together on a proposal for a joint-venture, and

2. My boss decided to leave me with his credit card so Hamish and I could have a 'night-cap'.

Worst boss moves in the world. A few stiffer drinks later and part of me wanted to launch at Hamish with his encouraging smile, but the other part of me kept thinking that he could potentially be a client, so I reminded myself to keep it professional. We called it a night and Hamish walked me to the hotel lobby lift and politely kissed me on the cheek… at that moment the lift doors opened, and guests walked out, and it was all a little awkward as I had dreamt some inappropriate action in the lift with Hamish, like they do in the movies. Hamish smiled and gave me a little wave with a 'I'll be in touch' as the lift doors closed.

Back in Melbourne, two weeks went by and I was still re-enacting the scene from the lift with Hamish, day-dreaming away, when my boss walked past my desk and commented, "You owe me one".

Puzzled, I wondered what he meant by this until an email came through later in the afternoon from… Hamish.

The email was business-like, which was disappointing, and he signed it off indicating that he would be flying to Melbourne next week and thought it important we catch up.

After thirty drafts, I sent my professional email back and scrapped the idea of ever marrying Hamish. I could never read the signs very well, but it appeared Hamish was putting his guard up as the emails leading up to his arrival became a lot less formal.

The week he arrived he suggested dinner at his favourite Japanese restaurant in South Melbourne. It was one of my favourites too, especially when work is paying. It's fancy, great atmosphere and delicious food. Twenty dress changes later and Stephanie dropped me off at his hotel lobby as Hamish and I were going to catch a taxi from there.

Stephanie nearly rammed her car into a bus as we peered into the lobby and saw him waiting there. She was speechless… and she would also like to come to dinner. As I leave her car, her last comment was, "Can he be any sexier?!"

Acting like an idiot, I waltzed into the lobby trying to pretend I hadn't seen him, and acted even more stupid when our eyes met. He gave me his sexy smile treatment. I melt and could hardly say "hi". He took my hand, and I was already in heaven, holding this sexy man's manly hand. He hailed the taxi with ease, as he was so manly and tall and solid, I was in awe and tried and make conversation, but I couldn't stop staring at him. Or looking around hoping everyone was looking at me with this hot guy on my arm and hopefully not saying "Gee, she's batting above her weight…"

We arrived at the Japanese restaurant. He'd booked us a table but because it's not ready, yet they suggested a drink in the bar. I couldn't agree more, so we head to the bar. Two bar seats perfectly positioned near the corner of the bar, it was dimly lit and away from the other tables. Hamish offered me my seat and I went to sit down. Because I was wearing hot-fitted black biker jeans – which are apparently a little slippery when you're talking to your future husband and go to sit on the bar stool that swivels and is slippery – I went flying off the other side of the bar stool and crashed to the ground, hitting my head on the bar on the way down. So, I was slightly hurt, could possibly be concussed, but I got up, with the help of Hamish, who was in shock, I laughed it off as if nothing has happened and continued on with my story. Gulping down my glass of champagne...

Finally, our table was ready, which was three levels up. Hamish asked if I was comfortable with him ordering, and I was just bedazzled by him so I couldn't care less. The conversation was flowing, there was a little hand holding and leg rubbing going on under the table and even a few sneaky kisses on my cheek and, overall, I was feeling pretty happy. I could keep this very professional – not. Entrée arrived, there was even a chopstick moment when Hamish served me some sushi, little did he know I couldn't actually use chopsticks. The main meal arrived, and another bottle of wine was poured, and I was on a high; okay I'm slightly tipsy, with slight concussion from the earlier bar stool stack.

Halfway through the main meal, I excused myself to powder my nose and was told the toilets are up another flight of rickety old stairs. I powered up those stairs to do my business as I didn't want to leave Hamish for one moment. As quick as I could, I checked I'm all in order, re-applied some lippy and raced back down the stairs as quickly as I could.

Only problem – halfway down in my stiletto knee high boots from New York, I missed a step and went flying down the stairs right past the opening to the middle section of the restaurant where Hamish and I were dining, hitting into the wall which was the only thing that stopped me from flying down the next set of steps. Waitstaff came from nowhere, as did Hamish, and a silence fell over the restaurant until the patrons realized I was alive. I didn't get up as quickly as I did after the bar stool incident, I was really hurting and trying to diagnose whether anything was broken, all whilst trying to keep my cool with Hamish.

Two large white serviettes later helped stop the blood trickling from a cut to my head and lip as I tried to convince Hamish I was fine. Sadly, my stunts for the night had shaken poor Hamish up and he was more concerned for my safety and how I was going to get home. I was more concerned how I was going to justify asking for another date with him next time he was in Melbourne and that hopefully I hadn't ruined everything business-wise for him and my boss. In the cab on the way home to drop me off at my place (Hamish did suggest hospital), he told me that there was never any 'business deal' with my boss, it was to take me out.

Of which my stocks had just crashed, literally, twice!

Chapter 21

Skinny Runner

Penny Curtis
To: Stephanie Thompson
Re: Negative awareness

Sometimes, I just can't understand why I can't see these things coming.

Stephanie Thompson
To: Penny Curtis
Re: Negative awareness

Okay, I'll be serious too then…maybe sometimes you're not meant to see it coming and you're meant to learn the lesson after the fact?

A girlfriend and I decided that we'd have a crack at joining in on a running function. Now, I know you're probably reading this thinking what is she going on about? Well, let me tell you, these running functions are for very fast serious runners.

My girlfriend and I are usually 'back of the pack' type runners; we like to have a chat and not push ourselves too hard, and in all seriousness, it's a good perve with maybe a glass of champagne at the end because we deserve it. We thought it would be better than speed dating, so we went along and surprised ourselves as there were some nice young fit gentlemen around our age who could run.

The next day, I decided to write a letter to the organisers for a terrific night and to see when the next running cross-country event was on. A reply came back with some humour, and hence a little email banter started with someone on the organising committee. I couldn't quite remember who it was from the night before, as I had carefully calculated that because I had run that morning, I could justify writing myself off. So, pretending I could remember this guy, I pursued an emailing relationship with him for about a week.

It then became a phone call and a text which meant serious developments. It got to the stage of organising to meet up on a weekend, however, because I was waitressing at the time it was difficult to co-ordinate. Eventually, he came through with the goods and rang me, saying he had tickets to see The Impressionist.

Stop. This is where I became cultured.

Of course, I said sure, I'd love to go. Never So of course I said sure, love to…I'd never heard of that movie before, but it sounded good, I said.

Need I go on? I call my cultured girlfriend Charlotte, and there was silence on the other end of the phone. The conversation went something like this.

"Charlotte, quick need your help. Skinny Runner has finally asked me out on a date to see The Impressionist, I have never heard of this movie."

(Long pause). "That's because there is no movie. It's an exhibition at an art gallery, think famous, think history, think never-mind."

Whoops! I think I failed history. And he hadn't said anything. So, Charlotte suggested I go over for a lesson 101 in Impressionists. We went through Rembrandt, Da Vinci who lost his ear, the most famous waterlilies painting. Over a bottle of sav I'd learnt more with Charlotte than I had a whole history class in my private school education.

On Thursday night I met Skinny Runner for dinner at Federation Square before the exhibition. So, we had a very romantic dinner sucking back noodles with salmon and sharing a bottle of wine. We walked to the gallery, and I was excited to start explaining to him that Van Gough cut off his ear and painted the water lilies. I have to admit, it was spectacular, and was made even more spectacular because he insisted on holding my hand the whole way around the gallery. It was a lovely night, and he was a gentleman. He walked me back to my car and kissed me goodnight, asking to see me again.

A couple of girlfriends and I signed up for a running course as we wanted to set ourselves a goal of achieving a marathon. Coming up a based level of fitness of nothing, we thought it time to get training considering the marathon was less than three months away. There were some lovely people at this running club.

Of particular note was this lovely guy who seemed to take a liking to me and fortunately I him. My girlfriend's and I were a little shocked as he was one of the best runners in club and I, well, I was actually the slowest however my girlfriends convinced me that opposites attract. Slow and steady wins the race?

Over the next couple of weeks, I was more dedicated to turning up to see Josh and run rather than focusing on my actual training runs. Josh was so lovely and would run with us and chat and laugh and keep us all entertained as none of us could speak whilst running because we were all gasping for breath.

How we even made it to the finish line of the marathon is beyond us. However, we made it, slowly, and the lovely people of the running club (who had already finished 2 hours ahead of us...including Josh) stayed to cheer us all on. Josh was very attentive.

We decided we liked the club and wanted to keep coming along for more 'social' training runs. The coach didn't mind as I think he wanted to encourage trying to even up the diversity of males vs females. Josh and I seemed to enjoy each other's company, although we were both so awkward with each. I was infatuated with him because he was so good looking, and I'm sure he thought I was a project ie take the slowest runner on a journey to try and improve her fitness.

Finally, Josh plucked up the courage one evening after training to ask me out for dinner later in the week. I tried to act cool however "yes" blurted out faster than Josh ran 100 metres. Awkward smiles from both of us and swapping of numbers we were looking forward to our date.

Leading up to the date, Josh texts a few times with some suggested dining venues. We agree to meet at a new dumpling bar in the city, which I was looking forward to until we ordered. I can't use chopsticks and I have never eaten ramen in my life. Josh seemed excited, so I did my best to embrace this new experience. I was finding it difficult throughout the night to control my slurping and clumsy noodle spooning and avoiding spilling it all over myself. Fortunately, the restaurant was dimly lit so Josh couldn't see the dribble streaming down my chin and onto my top. Let's face it dinner was awkward but there seemed to be an attraction.

I'd driven as I was up early the next morning for work, so Josh walked me back to my car and along the way we worked out his place was on the way home to mine so I offered him a lift. I park outside of Josh's flat, and he tells me had a really fun night and that he's really like to see me again. I couldn't agree more. So Josh leans across the middle console to give me a kiss, again I'm too quick to meet his lips and next thing my seatbelt has ricocheted me back into my seat. We laugh, he undoes my seatbelt and next minute we're enjoying each other's ramen noodles.

The next week, much to the run coach's dismay I am the first person to turn up to training. No sign of Josh. Concerned, I send Josh a light-hearted text and he responds that he has the flu. For the rest of the week I still turn up to run training but no sign of Josh. In a moment of Sainthoodism I offer to cook him some soup and deliver it personally. Josh is really appreciative and after work on the Thursday night I whip up some soup and pop over and deliver it.

His flatmate answers the door and tells me Josh is too sick to get out of bed. He takes the soup and then takes me down the hallway to Josh's room. I knock and Josh's voice tells me to enter. There he is all rugged up and looking very weary. He sounds terrible. I go to kiss him on his cheek and he quickly turns to kiss me on my lips. I pull back, concerned I may catch what he has. I sit halfway down his bed, ask him how he is and if he's feeling better. He thinks he's nearly over it. I tell him he sounds terrible and that I think he should go to the Doctor. I also offer him some soup. He says yes, I go and heat up some soup and bring it to his room.

Josh thanks me for the soup and I try and be a little romantic and sit next to him and feed him a spoonful of the soup. Our eyes met and there's this funny look in his eye. Next thing I know he's taken the bowl of soup and put it on his side table and reached for my hand and pulled his doona cover back and revealed a very stiff long part of his anatomy and was trying to force my hand to grab it and pull it. I jumped back in shock for three reasons (1) I couldn't comprehend how such a skinny runner could run with such a long piece of anatomy (2) that Josh had the audacity to grab my hand and ask me to pull at it when he was "sick" (3) he didn't want to eat my soup that I'd slaved over a stove for.

Stephanie Thompson
To: Penny Curtis
Re: Negative awareness

I know the lesson to be learnt in all of this…

Penny Curtis
To: Stephanie Thompson
Re: Negative awareness

Go on, I can't wait to hear it.

Stephanie Thompson
To: Penny Curtis
Re: Negative awareness

You should have been paying more attention to that famous running Shirvo. When he ran, I know you weren't cheering him on for his running ability.

Penny Curtis
To: Stephanie Thompson
Re: Negative awareness

No, you're right I honestly didn't see that one coming

Chapter 22

The Ghoster

Penny Curtis
To: Stephanie Thompson
Re: Ghosted

Have you heard this new term in dating?

Stephanie Thompson
To: Penny Curtis
Re: Ghosted

No. I thought it meant you'd been making clay on a kiln with Patrick Swayze

Penny Curtis
To: Stephanie Thompson
Re: Ghosted

Unfortunately, it's the complete opposite of that experience...

The blank above basically sums up what happened.

To this day, this date goes down in history as the best first date ever. Besides the fact I split my favourite jeans in the beginning as I stretched my leg to reach into his car.

Such a gentleman offering to pick me up at my place. I was a little hesitant giving out my address, but he was so lovely I didn't think it mattered. He was on time. I was excited to meet him as we'd had some only banter and a few phone calls, and we seemed to get along. As I hoiked myself up into his car I heard my favourite jeans split, but trying to act cool, I organised myself and we set off for brunch. Luckily, I was wearing a long draping top that hopefully would cover my split jeans with a gaping hole in my thigh.

Brunch was brilliant. We talked, we laughed and there was a little flirtation going on. At one point I excused myself to go to the bathroom and to check in on the situation of the torn jeans. Fortunately, my top saved me, and you couldn't see the damage.

Back at the date, our plates were cleared ,and we continued to talk and laugh together. A while later the waitress came up to us asking us if we'd like anything else. We decided on a glass of wine. Then a little more to eat. It was late afternoon and a few wines later my gentleman friend dropped me home. As I discreetly got out of the car, thankfully remembering my pants has split, we decided we'd like to see each other again. I was excited.

He drove off never to contact me again. Maybe he did see my ripped jeans.

Chapter 23

It's Not a Movie

Penny Curtis
To: Stephanie Thompson
Re: Sinking ship

Sometimes matters are taken out of my hands and I can't actually control the situation

Stephanie Thompson
To: Penny Curtis
Re: Sinking ship

That's too cryptic for me, I've just come back from a 'long lunch' if you get my drift… pardon the pun but you started the shipping jokes?

Penny Curtis
To: Stephanie Thompson
Re: Sinking ship

I know you're drunk, it's every day this week….I think I need a drink after last night's debacle

Stephanie Thompson
To: Penny Curtis
Re: Sinking ship

Oh yes, do tell how did you go with Aye Aye Captain?

Disastrous. A friend of mine had rung me up that morning and asked me to do her a huge favour and join a 'friend' of hers for dinner as she couldn't make it. A little hesitantly, I agreed to help her and her friend out. About an hour later I received a text from my girlfriend's friend Michael, and that he "requested the pleasure of my company for dinner". He provided the details, and of course I didn't really read them correctly.

I emailed Stephanie and told her about how I was helping out a friend's friend and was a little confused by the fact I was told it was just dinner, but Michael's text had indicated "cocktail dress and that we'd be meeting at 18:00 hours at Kitty Hawk". I googled Kitty Hawk and realized it was a movie, but was a little perplexed why I had to wear cocktail dress to the movies or why Michael hadn't responded to my query if we were meeting at Bondi Junction Gold Class cinema or Event Cinema at the Moore Park.

Feeling a little stupid in my cocktail dress heading towards either cinema, and because I still hadn't heard back from Michael, Stephanie saved the day by letting me know that although it was made into a movie, it was in fact the US

Naval ships that were in town and that Michael had probably invited me down for dinner to look at the ships. I'd much prefer to watch a movie than watch a US Naval ship.

Arriving down at the Woolloomooloo barracks I realised this was bigger than Ben Hur and, not only that, it had suddenly dawned on me that I had no idea who Michael was. Fortunately, he called me to give me his code to get into the barracks and told me I was to walk to 'his ship' and he'd meet me at the top of the gang plank. Was this guy serious? I finally managed to strategically walk in heels and my tight black cocktail dress across copious amounts of ropes in the dark to find two sailors saluting me at the bottom of the gang plank. Not sure what to do, I salute back which I don't think was correct as I have nothing to do with the Navy. Both these sailors helped lift me onto the wooden plank which was at a severe angle not helpful for stilettos.

On reaching the top, Michael was there, and weirdly presented me with a massive bunch of approximately 50 long-stemmed red roses. And all I could think was my friend must be setting me up. All just for walking up the plank? Too easy! I explained how I was happy to help out our mutual friend as she couldn't make it and then Michael escorted me along the ship's bow as all the sailors saluted as we walked past, and Michael saluted back. Extremely weird if you ask me. I am in hysterics. It's the United States of America Kitty Hawk, which is apparently a pretty significant ship, and we've been invited to dinner on her.

Madness. As we sat down at a table for 12, looking around I saw a number of other naval officers with lots of gold stripes and military badges tattooed across their starched white uniforms. One gentleman leaned in and asked me how long Michael and I had been seeing each other. He and his wife were a little taken aback when I responded with "approximately fifteen minutes". We all laughed, awkwardly.

As the evening continued, I realised that Michael was quite significant in the Royal Australian Navy and sadly, I also realised that Michael had told everyone we were an item. As the band started up, Michael asked me to dance, and the rest of the table joined us. Before I could try speak to Michael he flung me around – aka dancing with the stars style – and now I was dancing with another gentleman from our table.

After far too long dancing on concrete in stilettos, the ladies of the table were given a tour of the Kitty Hawk by one very attractive sailor of whom I wouldn't have minded if he had have been Michael. The ladies were bundled into a lift and taken up to the flight deck where there were fighter jets and helicopters. Women threw themselves at the fighter jets, taking selfies of themselves next to these gorgeous young sailors. All I could think about was how I could fly one of these fighter jets to get me out of this situation.

I should have thought harder or googled 'how to start a fighter jet' to get myself out of this pickle, because on our return Michael's table had organised a car for all of us to go out for more drinks and dancing at an establishment where one of the US Navy Sailors was also a DJ. We arrive at the establishment and I was standing with Michael when he started saying how beautiful he thought I was and that he's looking forward to starting this relationship with me, and how lucky he is that our mutual friend set us up…

Um, about that… I thought my friend was going out with Michael and I was just filling in for the night. On that note, I decided to dance myself into an oblivion and call our mutual friend the next day. I thanked Michael for a lovely evening, and he said he'd call me tomorrow, much to my dismay.

When I called my friend the next day, she exclaimed she had set us up. She said there was no way she could stand attending a function like that, plus she thought Michael was quite boring and not her type, but she had been desperate to find him a date and thought I was the best person to cope under those circumstances.

Unbelievable. Firstly, what a great friend. But secondly, giving that poor guy false hope.

Chapter 24

Sweaty Hands Flatmate

Penny Curtis
To: Stephanie Thompson
Re: Sweaty palms

Maybe I'm a clean freak?

Stephanie Thompson
To: Penny Curtis
Re: Sweaty palms

You're very tidy, but I wouldn't go that far.

Penny Curtis
To: Stephanie Thompson
Re: Sweaty palms

Do you think I cut this guy off too soon?

A girlfriend of mine moved into some share accommodation with two blokes as her flatmates. On a regular basis we would have a dinner at their place which was great fun. I got along well with both flatmates. Both very funny guys and both a great support to my girlfriend.

A few months went by and one of her flatmates started to act a little funny around me. We discovered he liked me and wanted to ask me out. Eventually he plucked up the courage to ask me out on a date to the movies which I thought was sweet, so I agreed.

On the afternoon of the movie date, I knocked on their front door and my date answered. I was nearly bowled over by the powerful scent of aftershave he'd obviously sprayed all over himself. Awkwardly, we'd gone from friend of your flatmate to a date scenario and this poor guy wasn't coping.

We stood at the open door for what seemed like an eternity, and I broke the silence by indicating are you going to invite me in or are we going straight to the movies? He was a stunned mullet. Finally, he agreed it was best to start walking to the movies. I was getting the feeling that my girlfriend flatmate had never been out of his flat before nor had he been on a date.

On the way I started talking and asked him what we were going to see. No response came back, my date was concentrating so hard that he then moved me to the inside of the pavement so he could walk on the outside. He explained he'd done this to protect me from being killed by a car that may be out of control and hit us. What a gentleman.

I continued the conversation with my protective date and started to ask him about his life. His response was that I now needed to hold his hand as we crossed the lights as it was very dangerous. Was this guy for real? Was my girlfriend trying to stitch me up? I explained I was perfectly capable of walking across the road and thanked him for his kindness. The lights gave us the green man to walk but my date did not. I stopped halfway through the crossing and looked back at him.

"Come on!" I encouraged. He shook his head.

"What's the matter?" I asked slightly annoyed with his behaviour.

"You need to hold my hand," he said not looking me in the eye. I tried to reason with him that I didn't need to hold his hand and that all of this commotion was unnecessary and could we just get to the movie.

"No, not unless you hold my hand," he said forthrightly. In my mind I'd already walked back to my car and driven home, but because he was my girlfriend's flatmate I didn't want this coming back at me and ruining everything for her.

"Oh, for God's sakes, I'll hold your hand across the street" I exclaimed.

He grabbed my hand slipped but it slipped out. He reached for my hand again, we sort of connected but then halfway across the crossing my hand slipped out again. I realized his hands were sweaty. We made it across the crossing, and I proceeded to remove my hand from his which was relatively easy to do as it just slipped out. He wasn't happy with this.

"You need to hold my hand the whole way to the movies," he said.

I politely explained I agreed to holding his hand at the crossing, but I was not prepared and felt it was unnecessary to hold his hand all the way to the movies and no doubt he'd then suggest throughout the whole movie. He didn't seem to be taking this very well.

"I just want you to hold my hand," he explained.

"No, it's not necessary," was my response.

I then gave him the ultimatum that he either drops the holding hands situation and we continue with our date to the movies, or I leave. He didn't like any of these suggestions, so I made the decision for us both.

I left him there in the middle of the street. He could hold his own hand home.

Chapter 25

Sprung Nurse

Penny Curtis
To: Stephanie Thompson
Re: The Fraud

Why do people have to lie? Do they not know it's a very small world out there?

Stephanie Thompson
To: Penny Curtis
Re: The Fraud

How good looking was he vs his intellect?

Penny Curtis
To: Stephanie Thompson
Re: The Fraud

Okay, on a scale of looks a ten. Intellect, maybe a two.

Stephanie Thompson
To: Penny Curtis
Re: The Fraud

And that, my friend, is your answer.

I was never going to be a professional triathlete. But I loved turning up to training, doing my best, then socialising afterwards because most people in the club were just great fun to be around.

After one hectic training week, a few of us decided to meet for a Sunday afternoon drink in St. Kilda. It was a beautiful spring day, and we were excited to catch-up outside of training.

My two friends from training were already there. One was anorexic and barely turned up, and when she did, she was nearly got blown off her bike or looked like she was about to die when she was running. My other girl was more along my lines, turning up to training for the more social aspects. Some guys from the club had also ventured to the bar which was great to see. Unfortunately, though, for Anorexic one drink and her other personality would come out of flirting with every guy and forgetting that she was actually here with us.

At one point we helped Anorexic into a taxi and then retuned to the bar.

I went to order my drinks. A guy smoothly walked up to the bar and started talking to me. I was clearly in shock, someone as good looking as him talking with me seemed too good to be true. My drinks were ready, and I didn't want to stop talking with him, so I told him to come over if he wanted to join our group.

I returned with my drinks to my friends, positioning myself so I could still see this incredibly good-looking bloke, and every now and then I'd catch a glimpse. I told my friend the story, she too stole a glance and at one point started to hyperventilate whilst trying to tell me he was coming over towards us. Pretending I had no idea he was on approach, I skolled my champagne and looked up to find him standing next to me.

"Oh, hi," I smiled. His name was Nathan, and he was a triathlete and a doctor. Double win. He was polite, bought me and my girlfriend another drink, then left as he had an early shift in the morning. My girlfriend glared at me, waving her mobile phone, alluding that I should ask for his phone number, but I was terrified, he was way out of my league. Fortunately, he was polite and gave me his number to call him. I watched as this amazing specimen walked out.

A few weeks later, I was at an afternoon BBQ and my phone buzzed. It was Nathan seeing if I'd like to come over for a drink. I'd already had a few drinks and didn't want to be tipsy if this was meant to be our first date (although it didn't seem to add up to a first date since I was being invited to his place for a drink). But I decided, who cares. I jumped into a taxi and arrived at his apartment block. It was a serious-looking apartment block, so much so it took me a while to work out where the front gate actually was. There also didn't seem to be a door buzzer either. Nathan had text me his address, so I knew his apartment block, but there were no unit numbers. I text him, and he replied saying just push the gate. But I seriously couldn't push the gate open. Looking around, no-one was watching so I thought I would scale the fence, which was a few metres high, in my skirt. I climbed the fence then fell over the top into a hedge on the other side.

When I finally knocked on his apartment door, Nathan answered in white Kelvin Kleins – and nothing else on. My heart skipped a beat as he invited me in, plucking some of the hedge out of my hair and asking if I'd fallen over.

"No, no, it's very windy outside, must have got caught up in my hair."

His apartment was filthy, but I didn't really care about that I was taken aback by his very healthy physic in his boxers. Trying to distract from the situation that was in his Kelvin's, I turned my attention to the fish tank in his living room. It was amazing.

I'd never had sex on a fish tank before. I can't say I recommend it, however, if the bloke who has invited you over has a fish tank in his apartment and is extremely hot, then I say go for it. And that we did. The fish seemed petrified, but it was definitely an experience I would be happy to repeat with Nathan again. Afterward, we were sitting on his couch, which was filthy, and he poured me a wine. He wasn't very talkative but made said he'd had a tough few shifts in emergency at the hospital he worked at. Apparently, he worked at the Alfred Hospital. I asked him if he knew my friends who were husband and wife and both doctors. He said he'd never heard of them.

After I finished my wine, I had the feeling Nathan didn't want my company anymore, so I left. On my way out he kissed me and told me to call him as he'd like to see me again.

Stupidly, I believed him. A few days later, I sent him a text to see how he was. No answer. I thought it was best to leave it. At one point there were signs of life when he texted back how busy he'd been at the hospital. Then he invited me over for dinner on Friday night. Of course, I accepted with enthusiasm. But on Friday afternoon he texted to cancel.

That weekend I was invited to a friend's BBQ. The husband and wife doctors that I knew were also there. I told them about Nathan, saying he was a doctor at the hospital where they worked. They shook their heads.

"Oh, do you mean Nathan Groves?"

"Yes, you know him!"

They turned to each other with a look of disappointment.

"Did you sleep with him?" asked the wife.

"Um, I might have," I said, half-annoyed at myself.

"Oh dear. Nathan isn't a doctor, he's actually a nurse at the hospital," she said.

"And not a very good one at that," chimed in her husband.

"But who lies about being a doctor?" I exclaimed.

"Someone who is very full of themselves," said the husband. "It's best you don't make contact with him, he's got a terrible reputation. He's ruined many marriages at the hospital."

Deflated, I wrote a note next to his contact details as an alert for myself to not contact Nathan ever again, regardless of whether he would be wearing his Kelvin Kleins or not.

A few days later Nathan text to apologise for messing up dinner, but how about a drink at his place tonight? I declined. A few weeks later, I was stuck in peak hour traffic on my way home from work around Albert Park Lake and I spotted Nathan walking around the lake. I'm not sure what overcame me, but I decided to pull over and text him.

"Hi, did you want a drink tonight?' I texted. I saw him get his phone out and look at my text.

"Love to, but I'm on duty now at the hospital and have surgery soon," he replied.

Unbelievable. I couldn't help myself, so I continued.

"I caught up with my friends who are both doctors at your hospital. They tell me you're actually a nurse."

I saw him look at his phone and shake his head. He texted back.

"Your friends are mistaken, it's a big hospital I studied medicine. I have to go into surgery. I'll call you later."

Then, for my final pièce de resistance I texted:

"No problem, Nurse Groves, enjoy your walk around Albert Park."

He looked at his phone then started looking around to see where I was. Then he sent a message.

"Don't text me ever again"

Too late, I've already deleted you. You fraud.

Chapter 26

PORTRAIT

Penny Curtis
To: Stephanie Thompson
Re: City meets country

I may have over-reacted...

Stephanie Thompson
To: Penny Curtis
Re: City meets country

That's not like you! How was your trip to the country? Did you meet that guy again?

Penny Curtis
To: Stephanie Thompson
Re: City meets country

Yes, we met up for morning tea

Stephanie Thompson
To: Penny Curtis
Re: City meets country

So, you didn't drink?!

Penny Curtis
To: Stephanie Thompson
Re: City meets country

I'm not sure what the rules are, however, I definitely needed a drink during that morning tea.

I'd been invited to an engagement lunch in the country a few weeks prior. The engagement party continued into the evening where we ended up at one of the local country pubs. My girlfriend and I were our usual sophisticated selves, trying to keep it together. Unbeknown to me, a guy from across the bar was checking me out and when it was my turn to organise yet another drink, not that I knew it was my turn by this stage, he approached.

As you could appreciate by this stage and a few drinks under my belt, everyone was looking quite nice, so Harry introduced himself and said he'd been watching me for a while (stalker alert) and he thought I was the prettiest lady here. Flattered, but let's be honest Hazza, it's not difficult to be the prettiest one here, there was a considerable amount of mutton dressed up as lamb.

Harry seemed lovely and not scary, so we exchanged numbers and I re-joined my group with more drinks that we didn't need.

Harry was keen and **over the next few weeks** kept the text messages going, as well as the occasional phone call. I was headed up his way again as my friend and I had signed up for a ten-kilometre fun run. Harry was keen to catch up, so I agreed to his suggestion of morning tea. I'm not sure why my girlfriend's whole family were involved, however her brother and his soon-to-be-wife and my girlfriend all dropped me off at the café and all saw him sitting on the balcony and all made a commotion. As I got out of their car and tried my best to not draw any further attention to myself and casually entered the café.

My heart was racing, as I couldn't see his face and was worried that all those drinks I'd had at the engagement were about to bite me. Harry stood up and greeted me with his oversized Akubra hat on. He was a lot older than I had remembered, but then again, I could bare remember a thing the night of the engagement party. It was basically a disaster from the beginning of the morning tea.

Harry must have been nervous because he didn't even manage to say "hi", he just dribbled. This then made me nervous. I tried the conversation starters. He was all awkward and kept spitting at me. Maybe he had a tooth problem? Thankfully the waitress came out to help break the uncomfortable silences we were experiencing within the first five minutes. In poor Harry's mind we were in for lunch as well, but I clearly told the waitress, "Just drinks".

Drinks came out in the nick of time to break the ice. It was slightly my fault, I asked Harry to tell me his story, so he took great pleasure in launching into his story starting nearly from when he was born. Too much information Haz! As my eyes glazed over, I saw my girlfriend, her brother and his soon-to-be-wife driving down the main street with all their windows down and the music blaring playing Dirty Dancing's "Time of my Life", screaming as they drove slowly past me.

"Hope you don't know those clowns," said Harry. I shook my head but inside I wanted to do the dirty dancing jump and fly over the fence and into their car.

Harry proceeded to say that he'd had the best time with me and would I like to be introduced to his family. A little startled, I told Harry I wasn't sure when I'd next be up, and perhaps it was too soon to be meeting his kids.

He leaned over, dragged what looked like a massive picture frame out of his bag and showed me what looked like a family portrait with Harry sitting in the middle of eight kids.

The first thing that came out of my mouth was, "Oh, are they all yours?"

"Yes, they're all mine, they all just have different mothers."

All I could think of was how I could possibly escape, right as Harry started telling me about each of his kids.

"Now, this little one here is Mary, now she's a real sweetheart, just like her mum. Good at sports too. Cheeky little character. And this one, well his name is Harry Junior, takes after his father, he got the looks. Everyone always comments how cute he is. Over here I'd like you to meet Sally, she's a little bit fiery but so was her mum...."

I was literally introduced to his entire tribe. Harry looked proud of himself, but I had to let him know that I wasn't up for being the ninth wife or partner, nor was I interested in becoming a part of his family. I also told him my lift was here, which it wasn't, and that it was lovely to catch-up but there was no need to keep in touch.

I'm not sure why Harry was perplexed. Perhaps I was the only woman that had stayed around long enough to be 'introduced' to his entire tribe. I'm not sure, nor did I care, I'd done my good Samaritan deed for the day. I raced out of the café, never to look back.

Penny Curtis
To: Stephanie Thompson
Re: City Meets Country

This time I can truly say a picture tells a thousand words.

Chapter 27

Speed Dating Situation #1

Penny Curtis
To: Stephanie Thompson
Re: Slim pickings

Not sure speed dating is where I'm going to meet the man of my dreams.

Stephanie Thompson
To: Penny Curtis
Re: Slim pickings

Surely, statistically, there would be one out of twelve that you liked? They say your chances are higher of meeting in that environment.

Penny Curtis
To: Stephanie Thompson
Re: Slim pickings

Well, someone forgot to give them the memo on these stats because it was a disaster right from the start.

Stephanie Thompson
To: Penny Curtis
Re: Slim pickings

Glad I cancelled at the last minute then....sorry!

Smart move, Steph. Clearly Steph knew something I didn't. Maybe she wrote the memo:

If you're male, have severe issues and look even worse in the dark, then this is for you.
If you're female, desperate and looking to be a shrink for a nutcase, then this is for you.

Steph cancelled at the last hour, so poor Emma and I bravely faced our speed dating evening together. We met for a Dutch courage glass of vino beforehand at the pub just opposite the speed dating pub. Emma told me a friend of hers recently got married to a guy she met through speed dating so we cheered to this encouraging outcome, perhaps it could happen to one of us.

As we sipped on our wine, we began to analyse the guys walking into the pub opposite who we were about to face. We had a few cheers and many more 'oh no' or 'hopefully he isn't part of the group' gasps. We finished our vino and entered into the unknown. We were trying to make ourselves laugh but really, we were terrified. An obnoxious lady greeted us, and Emma and I both agreed she was too rude to be the host.

She was the host.

The complimentary glass of champagne was flat, but when Emma complained to the bar staff, their response was 'take it or leave it'. We took it. The room was too dark for my liking and our over-bearing host told us to take our seats. Ladies were to sit up against the wall and apparently weren't going to move all night, whereas the blokes had to move every two minutes. On the table next to our flat champagne were two cards – one was labelled 'conversation starters', and the other was labelled 'my future' with a list of first names and tick boxes.

Who would have thought two minutes was a long time when trying to get to know the person opposite you? Let me tell you, when the person opposite you gives you absolutely nothing, or is full of himself, or can't speak English, it is excruciating. It went on for twelve guys, which I have summarised here:

1. Jerry – It was his fourth time speed dating, and he hadn't yet had anyone check his box. Might've been because his breath knocked me for six whenever he opened his mouth. X

2. Daryl – The first thing that came out of his mouth was, "Sweetheart, you might as well tick my box as I'm gonna tick yours. I noticed you as you walked in, the best out of everyone." When I didn't tick his box, he called me a slut. X

3. Barry – He was from Russia (was that really his name? Maybe it was short for Baryshnikov for shits and giggles) and could barely speak English.

He proceeded to whisper that he desperately needed a green card so would I be interested in marriage? No tick for you Baz. X

4. Mike: I'm not a fan of anyone that can't look me in the eye. Mike made me nervous. X

5. Wayne: He spoke about himself the entire time and mentioned he was just after sex and was I interested? *What, now?* How about no thanks and no tick for you ya sex maniac Waz. X

6. Paul: Started out well compared to the first lot. But after telling me how he hadn't had a date for years, he decided being aggressive would get him over the line. He questioned me on ticking his box because he was going to tick mine. Sorry, not working for me, Paul. No tick for you.

7. Graham: I'd seen and had contact with Graham previously on RSVP. Graham had clearly forgotten me, probably because Graham isn't the age he says he is. See you later, Graham-who-is-not-41-but-actually-56. No tick.

8. Frank: Not a great start when Frank sat down and the first thing he said was, "I can tell you're not going to want to go out with me." You're dead right Frank so that's a no from me, easy.

9. Liam: refreshing, not bad looking, great humour. I was just about to tick his box when he mentions,

"I'm married". Ah, fail. No tick for you or for your wife.

10. Tim: he gives me a quick snapshot of his political, religious and racist beliefs all in one, and I believe Tim needs to be locked-up. Tim is not safe. No tick for Tim, only a tick to prison for him.

11. Greg: nervous accountant, too short and a little sad, perhaps even a little sick in the head about women and the role he'd like them to play in his life. Greg needed help and didn't warrant a tick but an arrest.

12. And finally, the last fruitcake. Neil: when you ask Neil a question, he will start singing you a song. If you ask him another question, you get another song. Either Neil thinks this is Australian Idol or he is on something I need. No deal for you.

Exhausted, disappointed and with no boxes ticked for either me or Emma, we escaped back across to the other pub where we agreed we should never have left and drowned our sorrows with more wine.

Stephanie Thompson
To: Penny Curtis
Re: Slim pickings

At least you have eliminated another twelve blokes, although if you had to pick which one would you have gone with?

Penny Curtis
To: Stephanie Thompson
Re: Slim pickings

Probably Barry, the Russian, mostly because we couldn't understand each other, I think it would have been perfect. I've never been to Russia before.

Stephanie Thompson
To: Penny Curtis
Re: Slim pickings

I don't think Barry was going to take you to Russia, I think Barry was staying put here. On second thoughts, no need to choose anyone, they all sound disturbing. You need to give honest feedback to the host, in future the invite should read, "Only crazies need apply".

Penny Curtis
To: Stephanie Thompson
Re: Slim pickings

I'm done with speed dating.

Chapter 28

Fired on a Boat

Penny Curtis
To: Stephanie Thompson
Re: You're fired

This was definitely one situation I didn't see coming

Stephanie Thompson
To: Penny Curtis
Re: You're fired

Even I'm confused to be honest

My boss, who was a little crazy, sent me an invitation to drinks on a friend's boat for Saturday.

I had seen the guy once before – he had worked with our agency. It was awkward because my boss wasn't very nice, and I felt this was just a token invitation. But I decided to go, mostly because I didn't want to lose my job.

It was the most beautiful summer afternoon, perfect for an afternoon on the boat. I swung past my boss's house in an uber, and she appeared in what looked to be ball gown. I wasn't sure what memo she'd received, but that outfit wasn't gonna work on a boat.

On the way there, she started telling me a story about her and the boat owner. It sounded like she expected him to propose to her tonight. It seemed strange as I don't think I'd ever seen her go out alone, let alone with someone. The uber dropped us off at the Spit and we walked across to the marina to meet the other guests.

We exchanged polite pleasantries, and I noted that no one seemed to know anyone else except the guy who owned the boat. We were helped onto the boat, there was a briefing, and then the first champagne cork popped. It was all very weird.

As we motored out of the marina, I positioned myself away from my boss and sat with this lovely couple and started a conversation. We tried to work out everyone's connection. At one point they asked me how long the boat owner and I had been going out for. I was a little perplexed. To clarify the situation, I pointed out my boss in the ball gown and said, "Don't tell anyone, but she's hoping for a proposal tonight. She just invited me along." They were stunned, but I didn't think any more of it.

A few ladies were downstairs in the gully helping prepare nibbles, so I went down to help. These ladies were really lovely and a lot of fun, they made me feel welcome. As we prepared a few bits and pieces, the conversation turned to me. Again, the same conversation popped up. How long had I been dating the boat owner? I must have gone red in the face as they started laughing, and one woman put her arm around me, telling me not to worry.

"No, no, you don't understand," I tried to explain. I proceeded to tell them in a whisper that my boss, the one in the ballgown dress, was totally fixated on the boat owner and was expecting a proposal from him tonight. They all looked as stunned as me. I then told them that if my boss hears any rumours that he and I dating I could lose my job. They looked terrified. We tried to plot what to do next.

Meanwhile, my boss was up on the deck trying to engage the boat owner with her conversation, which he didn't seem very interested in. So, she tried harder. And drank more. Sadly, it wasn't working, as the boat owner turned his attention to me. My boss turned and gave me a look of death, so I excused myself, turned around and headed back downstairs.

Moments later, I turn around and see the boat owner behind me smiling at me. The other ladies were cleaning up and watching the whole scenario unfold. When one of them piped up to the boat owner and asks how he and I know each other.

As I went to say, "I know him through my boss", he said "Don't you know, we're an item."

Oh lordy, I rolled my eyes and laughed to let them know he was joking. But he wasn't.

My boss tried to come downstairs but struggled as her ballgown was too puffy. Finally she pushed through and nearly fell into the kitchen. She studied the situation then glared at me.

"What's going on here," she tried to ask sweetly, but she is furious.

"Nothing, I was just heading back upstairs," I replied, trying to push my way past her and started up the stairs. Then the boat owner declared we're an item. My boss grabbed the bottom of my dress as I was halfway up the stairs and pulled me back down. In a rage, she grabbed me by the throat and pushed me against the wooden door. The other ladies are screaming. The boat owner was sprawled out on the sofa watching. Thankfully, one of the crew came to my rescue along with the man from the first couple I met. They both pulled her off me as I gasped for air. I tried to tell my boss I have never met this guy in my life! The boat owner doesn't help by telling my boss he had made a mistake and we're not dating – but adding he would like to date me.

My boss yelled at me that I'm fired.

In shock, I launched up to the deck, only to realise I'm too far away from the marina to swim back so late at night. The crew and man that rescued me organised a water taxi not just for me, but for all the other guests except my boss. Thank God, it didn't take long to arrive. We bailed as quickly as we could, with everyone being very supportive of the situation I'd just experienced.

As we pulled away, the boat owner yelled out.

"Call me!" he shouted. My boss pushed him over the side of the boat into the dark water.

Chapter 29

DRIVING RANGE

Penny Curtis
To: Stephanie Thompson
Re: Driving me crazy

Why do men think it's ok to tell you how to do something when you're actually doing okay?

Stephanie Thompson
To: Penny Curtis
Re: Driving me crazy

It's just a male thing, you know, dates back to the cave years trying to be the hunter.

Penny Curtis
To: Stephanie Thompson
Re: Driving me crazy

Imagine us telling men what to do.

Another favourite activity of mine was playing golf. One night a week after work I liked to take myself off to the driving range to hit a few golf balls and unwind from the week. There was always a nice vibe in the evening at the driving range. I'd been consistently turning up on a Friday evening, most times finding myself in the same bay. I noticed the guy next to me also seemed to be consistent, too. We struck up a conversation between shots. Towards the end, we politely mention to each other, "See you next week".

Over the next few weeks, we seemed to have coordinated arriving at the same time, talking golf and enjoying each other's company. So much so, he plucked up the courage to ask me out on a date. Guess where? The following week, right here at the driving range. How could I resist?

The following week, I made a little more of an effort with my appearance and met him at the ball dispenser. We walked to our bays and worked out the best way to play a game between us. There are flags on the driving range with different distances on them, so we decide to aim for those and score points. All seemed to be going well, I was playing well and hitting my targets. He started off well but was soon missing his targets.

When I missed a shot, he couldn't wait to tell me what I was doing wrong. So, I'd thank him for his wise words, and focus on what I'd been practising with my golf coach (which wasn't him). He missed again. I hit my target. He decided to give me more advice on what I was doing wrong. This continued not just for my bad shots, but for every one of my swings. He then came into my bay, invading my space to tell me what was wrong. At one point he had the audacity to stand behind me – right up against me – and explained how I should hold my club. It tipped me over the edge. I counted how many golf balls I had left, hitting them as quickly as I could so the date could end. Then he told me I was swinging too fast... *there's a reason for that, bozo!*

Finally, I'd emptied my basket of golf balls and I was done. He was counting up our scores, I'd clearly been more accurate but somehow, he had won. Of course, he did. He suggested another basket each and mentioned that I could do with the practice. I had to bite my tongue. I said I had a good time and thanked him, but I really needed to get going. As we walked out together, he continued to tell me what practice I needed with my golf swing and that he was happy to help me. He even offered that perhaps we could try another date, this time actually on the golf course, which he mentioned would help me even more. I was exhausted from his help and decided that we could possibly look at something like that once I had improved my golf swing. He agreed.

Chapter 30

Milk pudding PT

Penny Curtis
To: Stephanie Thompson
Re: Lazy PT

How am I meant to get motivated if my personal trainer is lazy?

Stephanie Thompson
To: Penny Curtis
Re: Lazy PT

How much are you paying him?

Penny Curtis
To: Stephanie Thompson
Re: Lazy PT

Enough to warrant him to do a few push ups himself!

Stephanie Thompson
To: Penny Curtis
Re: Lazy PT

Well, he must have been good looking for you to fall for someone like that.

Penny Curtis
To: Stephanie Thompson
Re: Lazy PT

True, but I think I stopped at his eyes and ignored his gut.

I've never been one for the gym, I prefer the great outdoors. However, I'd been reading an article about how as women get older their bones become brittle and break into pieces more easily. I decided I should overcome my fear, purchase some appropriate active wear and buy a membership to my local gym.

As part of the membership, I received a free assessment which I didn't particularly want to do – and the results were enough to make me want to cancel my gym membership. Apparently, I had the stretching ability of a seventy-year-old. I didn't need to hear that. The only good thing was the fact they lined me up with Byron, my new personal trainer.

Byron had a very nice face, the type of beautiful blue eyes that you got lost in when he was yelling at you to give him 20 more push-ups, a slightly round stomach for a personal trainer, and very skinny, but muscley, legs. I didn't realise he was a little older than me.

During my gym sessions, I noticed Byron seemed to always be eating. He explained to me about protein and its benefits, so I assumed he was on the egg whites. Three months into my gym journey, after one painful gym session, Byron asked me out. I thought it was a little odd as I didn't really think my beetroot face and the fact I was trying to hide my guts with my oversized active wear was really a turn on. But I was flattered so I accepted his gesture.

He suggested a movie at his place, and, a little awkwardly, I agreed, worried that if I didn't he would make me do an extra set of everything during class. Arriving at his place on the Saturday evening, I wasn't expecting too much but he welcomed me into his place and he immediately took me into the kitchen. Did I like milk pudding?

He pushed a bowl towards me before I could explain that I didn't actually eat milk pudding. I noticed his own bowl was overflowing as he walked to the loungeroom and grabbed the remote to start the movie. I followed him to the loungeroom. His place smelt like wet clothes.

The movie started, but all I could hear was the clanging of Byron's spoon scraping the bowl as he polished off his pudding. Sitting at one end of the couch with him at the other, I felt like he didn't even know I was there. Then, without looking at me, he asked if I could get up and get him another service. Odd. I tried to make a light-hearted joke about getting to know each other first but he was so focused on the movie, he didn't acknowledge my comment. I sat there for a while, considering my next move. He went to grab his bowl then realised I hadn't re-filled it for him. Without taking his eyes off the movie he rolled off the couch, walked backwards, sat on the kitchen barstool, pulled the milk pudding towards him and dipped his spoon in and ate away. This went on until he finished the entire pudding.

Realising I was babysitting someone who was never going to make much more effort than this, I decided to leave. He was still looking the spoon and watching the movie as I closed the door behind me.

The next day I cancelled my gym membership.

Chapter 31

Anyone for Pimms?

Penny Curtis
To: Stephanie Thompson
Re: Foot fault

I have officially been put off tennis.

Stephanie Thompson
To: Penny Curtis
Re: Foot fault

But you love tennis, what happened? I thought it all seemed like a great idea.

Penny Curtis
To: Stephanie Thompson
Re: Foot fault

So did I, it was my idea to play tennis as a first date. I wanted to mix it up.

Stephanie Thompson
To: Penny Curtis
Re: Foot fault

Did you at least let him win one set?

We both had tennis as a common interest and a considerable amount of our banter was around it, which made me think a hit of tennis would be an ideal first date.

Daniel was in agreement, and our banter continued leading up to Thursday night's game of tennis, when he said he used to coach tennis. This put me in a slight panic that I'd over-stepped the mark, although I thought my competitive streak might see me through. He played up his ability – so he should, he was trying to impress me.

I couldn't have asked for a more perfect evening. It was daylight savings, a warm balmy night as I left work on time and made my way to the tennis courts. Daniel texted to confirm he was on his way too and was looking forward to our date. He left a smug remark about if he won, I'd have to shout him a round.

Once I arrived, I realised if I lost the match we would have to go elsewhere for a drink as this tennis club had no actual club, just a reception where you paid for your court, and if you were lucky, you could get a cold drink of lemonade from a fridge that looked like it was about to break down.

Waiting on the tennis court, I thought I should run through some warm-up exercises and have a few hits. I was feeling good, and it felt good that this was a different first date that Daniel seemed keen on too, rather than the usual drinks at a bar. A four-wheel drive came flying into the carpark,

Daniel got out and gave me a wave. He was in Wimbledon whites and sporting two tennis bags that held quite a few racquets. This guy was serious. I was impressed.

Daniel seemed quite animated (I took this to be first-date nerves), he gave me a quick peck on the cheek and asked if I'd like to serve. Of course. He took out a racquet and tapped it on his sneakers like the pros do. He waddled off down to his end of the court and squatted and swayed ready to receive my serve.

Whoosh!

"Out," he shouted, on a serve that I was sure was in. He confirmed with his racquet it was wide. Not convinced, I went continued to my second serve.

"Out!"

This time it was definitely in.

'Okay, I'll give you that,' said Daniel, waving his racquet at me. I didn't even make it through the next serve when he jogged up the side of the court and sat down on the seat, patting the space next to him.

"Is this a tactic to put me off my game?" I asked.

"Relax, we've got all night. Come and have a drink with me, we can chat."

I was a little uncertain. I mean, it's the first time we've met and he's interrupted our game. I reminded myself to be open-minded, but as I got closer, I saw one of his tennis bags was full of beer sitting in ice. At least he was organised, he must have already known about the fridge in the club. Or not.

When I sat next to him there was a smell – a mixture of cigarettes and beer. Daniel lifted his sunglasses and smiled, but I could see his eyes were bloodshot.

Daniel was drunk.

He cracked a beer and handed it to me. I took it begrudgingly. Unimpressed, I said I was serious about having a game and I was more than happy to chat with him while we played. He didn't look impressed, but he obliged.

I was furious, so back on the court, I had him running and sweating like a banshee. We may as well have met at a bar considering he had already drunk half of it. So, I made him run for every shot, until he raised his tennis racquet as a white peace-keeping flag. He fell to the ground, claiming he'd had enough. It wasn't even half an hour into our date.

I stormed off, slammed the gate shut behind me and headed to my car. I heard him call out after me.

"Wait, I'm sorry."

Too late. I was out of there. As I drove up the side of the tennis court, Daniel was gyrating at the fence, waving his racquet at me.

First impressions count, and this wasn't very impressive.

Chapter 32

THE RED G-BANGER

Penny Curtis
To: Stephanie Thompson
Re: Mort-i-fy-ing

Mortifying.

Stephanie Thompson
To: Penny Curtis
Re: Mort-i-fy-ing

I'd say innocent.

Penny Curtis
To: Stephanie Thompson
Re: Mort-i-fy-ing

In front of everyone?

I met Ned at a friend's wedding. He was lovely, charming in fact, an absolute gentleman. We exchanged numbers and he promptly called me the following day and we chatted, ending with him extending an invitation for the following Saturday to a polo match.

On the Saturday, I had joined a few friends very early for our weekly run around the Tan and then had dashed off for my regular mani-pedi and waxing all in preparation for this lunchtime polo. Frocked up, I was picked up by Ned and a few of his friends and their partners. It felt like a whirlwind of a morning.

A magnificent day opened up, the sun was shining, and the sky was a rich blue without a cloud. Ned introduced me to his friends and tried to explain the rules of polo to me. Champagne flowed and the fancy chicken sandwiches with no crusts were going down a treat. I was in my element, I felt like I was floating.

One of Ned's friends had a gorgeous cheeky little son, Fraser, who followed Ned and I around. His parents said if Fraser was annoying us just to let us know. But how could he be, he was just too sweet. He'd even offered to carry my handbag, putting it down on a chair for me.

There was a break after the polo competition finished for them to set up for the presentations. All the patrons were allowed onto the field with their champagne to put the divots back in – very Pretty Woman. Ned took my hand, and we stomped the divots back in together near our marquee.

From out of nowhere, there was a scream. We looked over, and there was Fraser, who had clearly rummaged through my handbag, found the red G-string I had put in there after that morning's bikini wax, and put it over his head like a shield. Everyone in the marquee was in hysterics as Ned boldly removed the red G-string from Fraser's head and put it back into my handbag.

Inappropriate comments were flying from nearly every second male's mouth. As Ned handed me back my bag, I clung onto it so Fraser couldn't find anything else mortifying.

Poor Ned, I think he was in shock, as was I.

I didn't hear back from Ned.

Penny Curtis
To: Stephanie Thompson
Re: Mort-i-fy-ing

Serves me right. There I go again, sabotaging the situation.

Stephanie Thompson
To: Penny Curtis
Re: Mort-i-fy-ing

The little kid probably did you a favour and lightened up the situation amongst those snobs. I think it was hysterical and if old Nedstar can't accept your red G-string and thought it was highly inappropriate then I think Ned needs some help.

Penny Curtis
To: Stephanie Thompson
Re: Mort-i-fy-ing

You're right, it was innocent, and everyone else seemed to see the funny side of it.

Chapter 33

My name isn't Julie

Penny Curtis
To: Stephanie Thompson
Re: Have I got a speech impediment?

What's my name?

Stephanie Thompson
To: Penny Curtis
Re: Have I got a speech impediment?

Say my name, say my name – isn't that a song?

Penny Curtis
To: Stephanie Thompson
Re: Have I got a speech impediment?

You must have been a fly on the wall

Stephanie Thompson
To: Penny Curtis
Re: Have I got a speech impediment?

Oh, I thought so. How did your date go?

There's slightly more pressure, isn't there, when your best friend's brother goes out of his way to set you up with one of his good mates. During the week, I receive a text from Stan, the friend of Stephanie's brother, asking me out for a drink early Saturday night. I was a little hesitant as I'd have preferred a coffee catch-up rather than something with alcohol, but he came recommended, so I agreed.

On Saturday morning Stan sent another text asking me how my weekend was travelling and if I was still okay to catch-up early evening for a drink. I reply 'Yes, looking forward to it'. A few hours later another text came from Stan indicating that something had come up and would I mind pushing out drinks to about eight o'clock in the evening. Again, a little hesitant, but because he was a friend of friend, I agreed. Stan sent through details of the pub, and I replied, 'See you there'.

Stephanie's brother had given me a description of what Stan looked like, but when I entered the pub, I realised quickly that it was doing to be a little more difficult to spot Stan than I had thought. The pub was supported by one of the major rugby league teams and was awash with supporters wearing caps and singing their club's victory song.

I found myself a seat at a table towards the back and sent Stan a message to let him know I had arrived. Soon he popped up out of the blue and gave me a hug and kiss on the cheek – and he was extremely intoxicated.

"You look beautiful, Julie."

Huh?

"It's Penny, nice to meet you."

"Can I get you a drink, Julie?" Stan asks.

"Yes, Penny would like a drink, thank you?"

"What does Julie drink?" asks Stan.

"Penny drinks champagne," I respond, bemused.

Stan skipped off to the bar and returned with our drinks.

Conversation underway, and Stan apologised for being slightly (I'd say extremely) intoxicated, and that his rugby team got into the grand final for the first time since some historic number. I politely told him if he'd known this, we could have met up another time. But now I have to listen to Stan dribble on about his team in his boozed-up state.

And he continued to call me Julie. I asked if his ex-girlfriend was called Julie, but he didn't respond. So, for the entire date he called me Julie, which, of course, didn't last long, as I decided it was pointless sitting there being spat at by a drunk as well as being called someone else's name.

Stan seemed shocked I was leaving after one drink. But two seconds later was talking to another group of people standing nearby. They obviously didn't want to have a bar of soap of him either, because as I flagged down a taxi poor Stan came flying out of the pub, on an angle, and promptly tripped over the guttering and fell face first into it.

As my taxi drove off, I did look back to make sure Stand was okay. And all I saw was Stan trying to stand-up. He was fine.

The next afternoon Stan called. He started the conversation with "Hi Julie-".

Are you kidding me, Stan? He apologised for being so drunk and wanted to make it up to me with tickets to Cirque De Sole, he was hoping I would like to join him. Unfortunately, for Stan, I'd already been to the performance, and I wasn't sure I could sit through another wrong name scenario, so I said no thanks. Stan was upset but understood and left the conversation with "Ok Julie".

I sent Stephanie's brother a text asking him if he'd told Stan my name. His response was "Who is Stan?".

The guy you set me up with from your golf club!

'Oh, Stan, I barely know him. He's actually a Policeman, he said he'd help me get off a fine if I set him up with someone. I thought you'd be the best person to oblige."

Where did the Julie come from? I never did find out.

Chapter 34

Horse Race Commentator

Penny Curtis
To: Stephanie Thompson
Re: Giddy Up or Off

How could I not see this coming?

Stephanie Thompson
To: Penny Curtis
Re: Giddy Up or Off

Look, it's perfectly normal, a friend tried to set you up and you think they've got your best interests at heart. They don't know their friend is a fruit loop.

Wonderful friends of mine are always looking out for me and my best interests, in particular when it comes to finding a suitable suitor. On one occasion, we were having a fabulous time at the races in regional Victoria when they introduced me to an acquaintance of theirs, who was, in fact, a horse race commentator. You know, one of those people who yells out the horse's names as they explode from the barricade and follow them around the field until the end. Although I got a red flag when they described him as an acquaintance rather than a friend, I kept this to myself.

As the day continued, the horse race commentator and I exchanged numbers. He seemed intelligent, although probably a little too serious for me. He also lived in another state. Over the next week we started up a nice, light-hearted conversation.

One evening he text me to tell me he was commentating on a horse race later that night and that I should tune in to listen to him and tell him what I thought of his commentating. It was a rainy Saturday evening and all my plans had been cancelled so I thought why not, something a little different. I tuned in.

He texted me about what happens in the lead up to the race call. There was a lot of detail to consider, he explained, such as the number of starts the horse had had, its whole background, the owners, the jockey, the conditions of the ground.

But it was getting late, and just as he was about to call the race, I fell asleep.

When I woke, I saw my horse friend had sent numerous text messages to ask how I rated his call on the race. Whoops. I took myself off to bed, deciding to respond the next day.

He wasn't impressed. By the next morning I'd received barrage of quite aggressive text which I wasn't impressed with. He then started calling me but leaving these very weird messages like he was calling a horse race, and I was the horse.

Eventually, I rang and left him a message on his voicemail explaining that had been quite late and I'd accidentally fallen asleep and that if he let me know when the next race was, I would be happy to listen in.

When I heard back from him it was another voice message. Again, it was him commentating about us like a horse race. So I texted him, 'What's with your voice message?' and he responded with another voice message in his commentary style.

I'd had enough. I rang him and left a message saying it was nice to meet him, but I'd just like to leave things and best of luck.

For the next couple of weeks, I received random voice messages about us in his horse race commentary style. I saved one and shared it with the friends who had introduced us. They were horrified. Later, my girlfriend rang me and said she knew a few other girls who had all had the same experience with him. What a freak.

Chapter 35

Whimpering at a Wine Bar

Penny Curtis
To: Stephanie Thompson
Re: Online Far too early

Now I am going the opposite direction.

Stephanie Thompson
To: Penny Curtis
Re: Online far too early

As in, you're now batting for females?

Penny Curtis
To: Stephanie Thompson
Re: Online Far too early

No, you silly cow! I'm just getting toward the unsympathetic side of the scale.

Stephanie Thompson
To: Penny Curtis
Re: Online far too early

That's fair enough, I don't blame you. Is there anyone out there at all anymore?

Clearly not. I decided to hop back online dating as a recent friend of ours had just got married to a guy she met on RSVP. All I ever heard when I went out with her was "it's a numbers game," or, "you have to be in it to win it". After a few attempts I finally connected with a guy named Bernie. He seemed half decent, and we had a few things in common, so why not.

Why not? Well, possibly because when I met Bernie at The Wine Library in Woollahra, he was not the athletic-looking specimen that he put up as his photos, likely from his university days, you liar Bernie. Sitting in front of me was three-times-Bernie, but I reminded myself not to be shallow.

Thankfully, our waiter swooned on in and took our drinks order. He looked as nervous for Bernie as I did. Something was not right besides the fact he looked nothing like his online profile pictures. Two glasses of chardonnay down and Bernie was still very nervous and kept excusing himself to the bathroom. Appreciating the scenario, our waiter coordinated my next glass of chardonnay. I told the waiter to 'hold' Bernie's. When Bernie came back from the gents and his eyes were blood-shot. Christ, not another drunk, or worse a drug taker. It looked like he's tried snorting the cocaine from his eyelids.

"Is everything OK, Bernie?" I asked. "You seem a little unsettled, if this is too much we can leave."

With that, Bernie started bawling his eyes out and sobbing uncontrollably with diners looking on (probably looking at me as if I was some soulless bitch who had just hurt Bernie's feelings). On cue, the waiter placed my glass of chardonnay in front of me, thank God, because I wasn't sure how I was going to get out of this.

"Everything okay here, ma'am?' the waiter asked.

I nodded with a strained smile on my face.

Bernie then explained how he'd been dumped by his wife two weeks ago and that his wife was being a maniac and even her mother was involved and being cruel to him. Through his sobs he continued to spew out everything that had happened, meanwhile I was sitting opposite with a very unsympathetic clenched smile on my face, trying not to take sides. My head tilted slightly and on the odd occasion would nod in fake sympathy. Poor Bernie, he was a mess.

After my third glass of chardonnay, and as Bernie continued on through their sex life and how it was difficult for them to conceive because he was under enormous strain working in his dad's chemical engineering manufacturing plant, which emphasized with spit that he hated, I waved for the waiter to get us our bill. *Sorry Bernie, but enough is enough. You need to pull yourself together and get yourself some help, and I'm definitely not it.*

Drained and just under one hundred dollars later, I walked Bernie out with the stares of the other patrons on my back. Bernie leaned in and gave me a strangling hug and I could feel his tears trickling down my cheek. He said he'd had the best night, and he was looking forward to our next date.

How do I break the news to Bernie so he doesn't have an even further meltdown? So, I told Bernie that it's really sad with what's happened to him, but he really needs to go and speak to a counsellor and perhaps too soon for him to be online?

"Can we at least be friends?" Bernie asked between sobs.

As if by sheer luck a taxi pulled up and I jumped in as quickly as I could. As I drove off, I saw a hunched over Bernie sobbing all the way down Oxford Street.

Stephanie Thompson
To: Penny Curtis
Re: Online far too early

I don't blame you, Bernie needs to get a grip, that's out of control

Penny Curtis
To: Stephanie Thompson
Re: Online Far too early

The only funny part of it, was that a couple of days later I bumped into the waiter and he wanted to know if everything was alright as he thought he was a fruitcake, he mentioned a few of the patrons had been worried about Bernie's behaviour

Stephanie Thompson
To: Penny Curtis
Re: online far too early

Well, I am proud of you, you're not here to fix Bernie's issues with his wife that just dumped him.

Chapter 36

Corporate Surfer

Penny Curtis
To: Stephanie Thompson
Re: Hang 10

I need to stop falling for these guys dressed up in disguise as someone they're not

Stephanie Thompson

To: Penny Curtis
Re: Hang 10

It's not easy, but luckily you found out early enough

Penny Curtis
To: Stephanie Thompson
Re: Hang 10

Clearly, I forgot to take the 'salty sea' man test, my mistake

Out at yet another work function one evening, I was standing there holding onto a glass of champagne, not really interested in what was going on but pretending to be present. It was a networking function, and it was compulsory for me to attend as no one else from our company was.

Trying my best to put on a brave face, smiling my fake smile and counting down the minutes until the event is finally over, I stepped back into a dimly lit corner to try and escape, and accidentally bumped into someone. My drink spilled all over them, and as I turned, I saw a rather nice man dressed in his corporate suit and looking mighty fine. I fumbled my apology, trying not to make too much commotion and draw attention to us. He laughed and dabbed his jacket with my filthy serviette which was falling apart on him. I made things even worse by stepping back and tripping over a stand which had a dead pot plant perched on top of it. He grabbed the stand with one hand, and me in the other.

Thankfully, the corner was dimly lit so he was unable to see how red my cheeks were burning. After all the drama, we stood next to each other, and he asked me if I was trying to escape. I explained this was the hundredth event I had been to for my company, and no one usually talked to me anyway, so I felt it was a boring waste of my time. He agreed, indicating he was in a similar position. In fact, the company that put this event on was actually his company, but he didn't like the event either. I couldn't believe I'd put my foot in in big time. He asked me what company I worked for and I tried my best to ignore the question, changing the subject as quickly as I can.

We continued to discuss worldly topics and then got into the nitty gritty of life details. He had grown up surfing and was a professional surfer who travelled around the world.

Wow, amazing. He asked me if I surfed and I mentioned that I had tried it but wasn't very good (in fact, useless at it). He said I should come watch him surf sometime or drop into the international surf shop that he owned. And on that note, he handed me his business card, kissed me on the cheek and said, "call me and we'll do dinner". Not bad for what had looked like an absolute disaster! I called him a few days later and left a message but never heard back from him.

A few months later, I was heading to Noosa for a well-deserved holiday and couldn't wait to get on that airplane. Organising myself in my seat I looked up and saw the same guy walking down the aisle. As he approached, I looked down, pretending not to have seen him and praying he wasn't going to sit next to me. Anyway, why can't he afford business class if he owns that company? He sat down next to me and starts talking away as if we'd never met. A little confused I politely responded.

The plane taxied back, and we exchanged some polite chit chat about our holiday plans, it turned out we were staying at the same hotel. He was having a surfing holiday while I was taking a relaxing break from city life. Then I put on my headphones.

As the flight descended, he ignited the conversation again. He suggested I jump in his private car since we were going the same way, and obligingly I accepted. As we parted ways at the hotel, he gave me his mobile.

"Call me," he said, "and we'll do dinner."

A few days later, I was enjoying my book on the beach basking in the sunshine when a shadow came over me. I looked up and here was this guy with his surfboard. He started talking about my book, and gave the plot away, which didn't impress me. Who does that?

He talked to me as if he'd never even met me before, even though he'd met me twice! Before he left, he dropped me his card with his mobile and said the same line as before.

"Call me and we'll do dinner."

Was this guy for real?

Back at the hotel, I decided to Google him and his companies. That's when I discovered nothing stacked up. His name didn't come up as the owner of any business. His name didn't show on any search on social media. It all seemed very suspect.

On my final morning, I decided to enjoy breakfast in the hotel as I was avoiding bumping into this guy for fear of another business card thrown at me. But sure enough, he came wandering in and stopped at my table.

"Mind if I join you?" he asked.

"Actually, yes I do, I just would like to eat by myself thank you." He clearly didn't take no for an answer and went to sit down. Then he launched into the same life story. I excused myself, and noticed he was reaching into his wallet for his business card. I stopped him in his tracks and explained I had received many, and thanks, but I wasn't interested. He looked confused.

My car was ready to take me to the airport, and I was settling my bill when I noticed additional charges for items. Dinner every night at the restaurant, drinks in my room, and apparently, I purchased two dressing gowns. There was also an additional amount on there for drinks sent to room 105 – that guy's room! What the hell was going on?

The guy was a fraud, and he hadn't just tried it on me. The receptionist looked up other rooms and sure enough, the guy had tried to off load his dirty laundry on quite a few unsuspecting women in the hotel.

The police were called, I made a statement, and the hotel was kind enough to change my flight, so I wasn't out of pocket for this creep's deceit.

Stephanie Thompson
To: Penny Curtis
Re: Hang 10

I'm not sure he falls into the 'salty' man category to be honest; I think something else is going on.

Penny Curtis
To: Stephanie Thompson
Re: Hang 10

You're probably right, he was an odd character.

Chapter 37

THE ARBORIST

Penny Curtis
To: Stephanie Thompson
Re: Hugging trees

This online dating scene is a farse!

Stephanie Thompson
To: Penny Curtis
Re: Hugging trees

What do you mean?

Penny Curtis
To: Stephanie Thompson
Re: Hugging trees

I feel like the men have got their sister or best girlfriend to write their profile which lures you in.

Stephanie Thompson
To: Penny Curtis
Re: Hugging trees

In reality, they're not who their profile says, they are?

Penny Curtis
To: Stephanie Thompson
Re: Hugging trees

Not anywhere near.

Snow skiing is a favourite activity of mine, I've been skiing for years. In an ideal world I fall in love with someone that likes this past time too. This nearly occurred.

I'd taken off to Thredbo for a weekend by myself as I needed to get out of Sydney. The season had just opened with bluebird sunny days and fresh snow, always the best combination. One afternoon I was skiing one of my favourite runs because it was quite protected and not many people were there.

Catching the chairlift up this particular run, I noticed another skier was also regularly skiing the same run, and we seemed to be timing it so we caught the chairlift together. Eventually we plucked up the courage to talk to each other and we seemed to hit it off so much that we skied the rest of the day together. We swapped numbers and we ended up meeting in Sydney.

A famous movie by Warren Miller was showing as the local movie theatre and my new skiing buddy called me to see if I'd like to join him as he had two tickets.

Of course, I love these movies, produced at the beginning of every ski season. My Dad used to take my sister and me to them when we were younger. So I drove over to his place as we were going to walk up to movie theatre which was a short stroll from his place.

When I got to his place his flatmate answered the door on his way out. A brief conversation of polite pleasantries and he mentioned my date was inside. I showed myself in and was hit by this low hanging cloud of fog which smelt very much like copious amounts of marijuana. As I battled my way through the thick fog I came into the loungeroom and there was my friend, wrapped up in a blanket with a beanie on his head, smoking what looked like a joint.

Startled, I questioned my friend on his ability to get up and walk to the movies. As he fell off the couch and tried to stand upright, he indicated he was fine. He stunk. We walked to the movies, and he proceeded to sing whilst finish off his joint. When he spoke to me, he made absolutely no sense. When we entered the movie theatre it was evident my friend didn't have two tickets and he asked me if I could buy them. I turned to reply but he had fallen over and was scraping himself back off the ground. People were starring.

The security guy at the movie theatre came over and could obviously smell my date. I slowly sidled away from him as the security guard asked him step outside. I watched as he was escorted out and I proceeded to buy myself a ticket to the evening, entered a ski holiday competition and thoroughly enjoyed the movie.

To top it off, I won the ski holiday.

Stephanie Thompson
To: Penny Curtis
Re: Hugging trees

Please tell me you didn't feel sorry for him and invite him to your ski holiday.

Penny Curtis
To: Stephanie Thompson
Re: Hugging trees

No way, that would be a complete waste of a great ski trip.

Chapter 38

Family Jewels

Penny Curtis
To: Stephanie Thompson
Re: Family Jewels

How does this go so wrong so early?

Stephanie Thompson
To: Penny Curtis
Re: Family Jewels

I think you did the right thing to support a friend of a friend's friend

Penny Curtis
To: Stephanie Thompson
Re: Family Jewels

And it backfires on me...

Stephanie Thompson
To: Penny Curtis
Re: Family Jewels

You weren't to know, try not beat yourself up

A friend of a friend set me up with a guy who travelled a considerable amount for work. We had a few brief phone calls before he was in town for business and asked if I'd like to join him for a dinner. I'm not a huge fan of a dinner when it's a first date because I feel that's a long time to sit through if you're not really into the person. Considering it was a friend's friend I thought it couldn't hurt. How bad could he be?

We met at the restaurant and instantly something didn't feel right. I'm not sure what it was but I didn't feel comfortable. We exchanged polite pleasantries and the waiter came over to take our drinks order. He took it upon himself to order for the both of us. He ordered a Riesling. I don't like Riesling.

When it was time to order our meal, he again tried to order for the both of us. I decided enough was enough and stood my ground. Very politely, I smiled at him and explained that I didn't like what he'd ordered for me. He seemed very taken a back and explained he always ordered for women. I wasn't sure how to respond to his remark.

He seemed nervous throughout dinner. I wondered if I was holding him up from a business deal he was trying to secure. He spilt his wine, and he was perspiring a considerable amount, even though the room temperature was quite cool. All I kept thinking was for this date to be over with as quickly as possible.

Thankfully, he must have read my mind as he ushered over the waiter for our bill. I insisted I pay for my half as I didn't want it getting back to my friend's friend that I didn't pay my half considering I was never going to see this guy again. He refused to accept my half for the bill. Instead, he decided I was going to head with him back to his hotel where there was a wine bar, and we would continue the evening.

Considering this guy didn't take lightly to rejection I politely declined making up some excuse about work the next day. He didn't like this and tried to manipulate the situation, which I thought was odd behaviour. He started to express how he felt about me. We'd just met, so I wasn't sure how he could have developed these feelings so quickly. This was starting to get on my nerve now. I thanked him for dinner and his kind words, but it was time for me to catch a taxi home.

Waiting outside for a taxi, he was standing in front of me trying to convince me that I join him at his hotel.

"Thank you, but no thank you," I responded trying to not look at him in his eyes. He was much shorter than me and was trying to reach up to touch my face. As my taxi pulled up, he refused to let me get in. I tried excusing myself. He blocked the door.

Noticing that a commotion was going on the taxi driver took the opportunity to drive off. *Damn it.* I started ordering another one. As my date was begging me to join him at his hotel, I politely told him to please leave me alone and that I wasn't interested in continuing anything any further with him.

In a last attempt, he dropped his brief case and opened it up to reach in to pull out a long jewellery box.

"Here," he said. "I felt such a connection with you tonight, I know you feel the same way about me. Here, please I want you to have this."

He snapped open the jewellery box and there was this necklace with an oval picture of an elderly woman as the centre piece.

Was this guy for real?

Taxi number two pulls up and with his hands busy with the jewellery, I managed to scoot around and jump into my taxi, slamming the door shut and telling the taxi to hurry up and get me out of here.

Seriously, what a fruit loop.

Then I received a bombardment of text messages from this crazy guy.

The texts went from nice crazy to threatening crazy, at which point I blocked his number.

Stephanie Thompson
To: Penny Curtis
Re: Family Jewels

I'm not sure there's "nice crazy"…he's just crazy full stop.

Penny Curtis
To: Stephanie Thompson
Re: Family Jewels

Very true, I mean who gives the family heirloom to someone they've just met that night for the first time?

Chapter 39

Carbon Tax Lawyer

Penny Curtis
To: Stephanie Thompson
Re: Enviro

I thought going green might rid of my spell but I think that's taking me out of my comfort zone.

Stephanie Thompson
To: Penny Curtis
Re: Enviro

Sure, you watch David Attenborough, and you think he's your hero but I think that's the extent of your 'greenness'.

Penny Curtis
To: Stephanie Thompson
Re: Enviro

Maybe I should have paid more attention in science at school.

I came up with a theory because none of the other ones had been working. This new theory was to cut to the chase. No more endless messaging on the apps. This was empowering. Have enough online messaging to the point I felt they weren't a psycho, then boom, meet them for brunch. I liked brunch, it was quick and easy, and if I chose the restaurant, it could also be delicious even if the date wasn't.

Over the coming weeks I decided to test this theory out. Enter Forensic Carbon Tax Lawyer. In truth, I only really noticed the 'forensic' part of his title. Lucky for Mr. Forensic he was about to experience one of my favourite places for brunch. I'll admit there was a little hesitation on his behalf, maybe my theory was a little too quick for him (he tried the old theory of meeting for a drink instead).

Luckily, my favourite brunch cafe was walking distance from my house, but far enough that a date couldn't see where I lived. Running late and feeling a little dusty due to the incredibly big night I had the night before with the girls, I was able to make it on time but unfortunately Mr Forensic was already waiting at the table. In my mind I kept trying to tell myself, "be open minded, he could be the one," but then when I looked at him, gut instinct told me he wasn't. At least I would enjoy my bacon and poached eggs with avocado on sourdough to soak up the fun I had the night before.

Well, at least he had manners as he stood up to welcome me to the table. But he was quite unattractive compared to his photos, clearly taken a few years earlier. He was far too short for me, even though his profile had him taller than me (liar already), and he had very yellow teeth which I couldn't stop starring at. Like, super yellow, as if he hadn't cleaned them all his life. His hair was receding and had really dirty nails, but he was in a suit and tie which I thought was a little weird considering it was weekend brunch, but who am I to judge, I was hungover. But those teeth were ghastly, hasn't he ever heard of a dentist? Maybe it was a disease, poor guy.

Thankfully, the lovely waiter helped ease that uncomfortable awkward moment in the beginning when there's silence because no one knows what to say.

"Coffee?"

Yes! We ordered and started on the polite pleasantries. The only issue was, there were incredibly long pauses before Mr Forensic spoke. I wasn't sure if he'd finished his sentences, so as I went to jump in he continued talking over the top of me, but really I was talking over the top of him but didn't realise because I thought he'd finished his unfinished sentence. It didn't seem to be nerves, more like a stroke was about to occur.

Coffee arrived and we ordered food. I let him speak whilst I sipped on my coffee so that I could work out when it was my turn to speak. I made the unfortunate mistake of asking him what he did, and let me tell you, two coffees, bacon, poached eggs and avocado on sourdough toast down the hatch with (I'm sorry but I was hungover) an apple and cinnamon muffin later and then a glass of wine, my theory was putting me to sleep.

My brunch friend went on and on and on about his job and explained in detail the intricacies of the environmental impact we were all having and what this was doing to our planet. As he spoke, he asked me questions, but continued talking, clearly not interested in my viewpoint or answer. Not that I had one to give, of course, because I had absolutely no idea what he was going on about. As I inhaled another mouthful of my muffin and worked on my exit strategy, I scanned the room and locked my eyes with my boss and his family sitting at a table opposite us finishing up their breakfast.

Panic. I looked at Mr Forensic who was still talking to himself about some policy. Seriously, he had no awareness of how boring he was. And then, to add insult to injury, my boss came over to say hi and introduce his family. I stood up, making a fuss over his kids and commenting I didn't know they lived in my area. At that terrible moment, he asked if I was going to introduce him to my friend. My appalling response was, "He's not my friend."

"On that note, we'd best leave you alone," he said, and they exited stage right.

Meanwhile Mr Forensic who isn't my friend was still going on about carbon tax and then all my blood sugar levels must have aligned and I realised he was too boring for me and I needed this to end. The lovely waiter came past to ask if we'd like anything else. I said, "the bill," as tax man said, "a coffee". I politely explained that I had to get going as I had an appointment to get to, and maybe he could get a take away coffee. I think he was in shock.

The bill arrived and he smiled his big cheesy yellow smile and said, "Probably best we go halves". Whatever, hurry up. Of course, he tried to look like he could add up without a calculator, did his adding up theatre and came to the conclusion that we owed thirty dollars each which included a 'mild tip'. Embarrassing. The bill was paid, and he continued to talk about an economic carbon act that he was trying to pass as he sipped on his water. I, on the other hand, was half out of my seat heading for the front door.

He is bewildered as to why I was in such a hurry, and tried to jokingly say, 'It's as if you're trying to get away from me.' Ha! If only he knew. I was a few steps ahead trying desperately to walk to my car without seeming too rude with him dawdling behind and still talking. I reached my car and thanked him for meeting me for breakfast. He thought that was his cue to lean in and give me a kiss, which I avoided as I jumped in the car and slammed my door. As I was about to drive off, he held his hand up to his ear with that thumb and baby finger symbol and mouths, "Call me".

Sorry Mr. Forensic Carbon Tax Lawyer it's probably best you call yourself coz I ain't interested.

Stephanie Thompson
To: Penny Curtis
Re: Enviro

I don't think paying attention in your science class would have helped you on a second date with Mr Environment

Penny Curtis
To: Stephanie Thompson
Re: Enviro

No, you're right, in future no one in the sciences – they're all out.

CHAPTER 40

I THINK I'M IN HELL-I-TOSIS

Penny Curtis
To: Stephanie Thompson
Re: Bad Smell

This sort of feels like another one of those moments when your mum asks you if you've cleaned your teeth and packed your handkerchief.

Stephanie Thompson
To: Penny Curtis
Re: Bad Smell

You're always cleaning your teeth. In fact, you even have a travel bag in your handbag with your toothbrush and toothpaste.

Penny Curtis
To: Stephanie Thompson
Re: Bad Smell

Well, my advice… if you're mum isn't around then carry a traveller.

I'm not sure why I do this to myself, I think it's called 'definition of insanity' but I always want to give a guy a fair go. My general rule when dating it to not go for dinner on the first encounter. Unless he's someone so hot I know I'll never see again, and I can make exceptions to this rule. However, sometimes I get carried away because in my gut whilst talking with them I feel like I have this connection and I feel comfortable enough to meet them for a meal.

Time and time again, it doesn't work. Some of us are brilliant at texting and messaging but when you meet face to face - boom! It's all goes to shit. This was one of those moments…

I thought I'd be open minded and look beyond the Australian male, instead venturing off to Europe. Why not! Up popped Pierre. He had reasonable English and from what I could make out from his online pictures, he was also okay on the eye. There was my first mistake. Images that are too far away is a huge warning, but I chose to ignore it. Pierre's profile read well, and we seemed to have a lot in common. After a few messages and even a phone call, Pierre was giving me a good feeling, so I agreed to meet for dinner.

It was a beautiful balmy early evening and the restaurant that I had chosen was within walking distance from my place. As I skipped toward the restaurant, I started practising what little French I knew. I was early and positioned myself at the table so I could see what was going on in the restaurant in case I needed to make a quick exit. The waiter asked if I'd like a drink and I went for a glass of French Champagne. Sitting there pondering who was actually going to walk in I gazed around the early evening diners and realised we were surrounding by a sea of young families and their kids. No one really looking like they were enjoying themselves. I took another sip.

Pierre arrived much shorter than his bio online and a lot less hair too. He kissed me on both cheeks and then sat down and ordered a drink. Polite pleasantries started our conversation. He was nervous I had already planned my exit strategy knowing he wasn't the one. But as I took my next sip, I realised I needed to be open-minded for he could be a Prince of some chateau that needs restoring and I could travel between Sydney and Nice. Distracted by my own thoughts the next table jolted me out of my dream and back into reality. Their kid had decided that he didn't want any more of his spaghetti bolognaise and ensured his sister in the bassinette should wear it instead. Pandemonium broke out.

Pierre didn't seem too phased by any of this as he scanned the menu. I wasn't sure if it was the noisy kids, but there was definitely a ghastly stench coming from their direction. At one point I interrupted Pierre and asked him he could smell that odour. "No," he replied shaking his head looking around. We placed our order and continued our polite conversation. I noticed Pierre seemed to have a list of questions he needed answers to.

"Why did you break-up with your last boyfriend?"

"Oh, okay, well I guess it just wasn't meant to be."

"Is that a good enough excuse? It sounds to me like you didn't want to put much effort in."

Slightly alarmed at his response, I thought to myself I'm not playing his games and decided to agree with him.

"No, I guess you're right." With a roll of my eyes.

As the night dragged on, the smell seemed to be getting worse. The family beside us had paid their bill and left, and that table hadn't been occupied again, so it was just the Frenchman and me. I went to ask Pierre about his last relationship, and I was met with a combination of his reaction like he was having a fit and that smell crept further across our table. Pierre decided that only I should answer the tough questions about past relationships and that it was "none of my business to pry!"

Oh, here we go, he's probably married and she's at home waiting for him.

Soon I was running out of questions and patience with Pierre. The waiter asked us if we'd like dessert, and my response was "Non," and Pierre's was "Oui". And as he it, he sneezed across the table without covering his mouth.

There it was, oh dear God, that stench was him, the Frenchman. It smelt like a sewer. The restaurant was dimly lit so I couldn't really see the colour of his teeth, maybe he had forgotten to clean his teeth. It was a ghastly smell, so much so I barely ate my dinner. Pierre suggested a compromise for not having dessert of having one more drink. I guessed I could sit there for one last drink whilst his stinky breath sprayed across the table.

Excusing myself to freshen up in the ladies, Pierre stood up, lent in, and went to kiss me on my cheek, and there it was again – dead horse smell breath. I held my breath until I got to the ladies and exhaled. As I looked at myself in the mirror my friend and work colleague walked out of the toilet.

"Hey, so good to see you, what are you doing here?"

"A date from hell," I replied.

My girlfriend indicated that she and her husband were here with their kids, and she had seen me and thought that I didn't look very comfortable. It wasn't. I told her about his stench, so we Googled it.

We narrowed it down to what's known as halitosis, which is some dirty stinking fungal infection of the mouth from poor oral hygiene. I wanted to be sick. My girlfriend waited for me and then offered me a shot before heading back to the table with Pierre. We both downed a cock sucking cowboy and I strutted myself back to Halio the Frenchman.

"What took you so long?" asked the inquisitive snail. I had many answers that were totally inappropriate, but I decided to refrain from telling him and instead smiled sweetly and just mentioned I'd bumped into a work colleague. Thankfully, the waiter turned up with our last drinks and the bill. I can't really recall too much more of the conversation, as I was trying my best to avoid Pierre's breath. It was like a very bad dream. We sorted the bill and walked out.

There was the awkward moment when he thought we had both had such a great night. "Obviously we'll be organising the next date," he said. My taxi was coming round the corner, and I hailed it as I stepped off the pavement. "It was nice to meet you, however, I don't want to take things further."

With that, I slammed the taxi door shut and asked the taxi driver to step on it.

Five minutes later, Pierre was still standing outside the restaurant, dumbfounded. A text message arrived.

"I thought you liked my questioning?"

At that moment I want to text back, "No, I didn't, and nor did I like your breath," but I refrained. At least I seem to have a strong end game if I'm not remotely interested in someone, especially someone with halitosis.

Chapter 41

Speed Dating Attempt #2

Penny Curtis
To: Stephanie Thompson
Re: Radar

How come I can get a 'gut feel' when someone isn't right for me but when I like someone I can't tell if they're straight?

Stephanie Thompson
To: Penny Curtis
Re: Radar

I hate to admit it's not one of your strengths, but then again you were speed dating I am not sure how this guy even came into the equation?

It was pouring with rain on the Thursday evening, and I was very tempted to cancel on my friend who wanted to try speed dating via a cooking class. But I didn't want to spoil her fun, so I decided to commit, even though I'd rather have been at home in my pyjamas with a cup of tea.

Drenched, I entered the warehouse building which was in a suburb outside the city so I was intrigued to find out who would turn up to something like this. My girlfriend was already registering on the ladies' side – I mean really, why not just register together as it might spark a conversation prior to this nerve-wracking event. My girlfriend was beside herself with nerves so once we'd both registered, we received our complimentary glass of champagne which was actually French and thought this was going to be a good night after all.

Looking around the room, let's be honest, it was going to take a few more champagnes before anyone really caught my eye. There was a difference between the city speed dating guys and the suburban ones. I took another champagne as the waiter came past. It was a really awkward set-up in a kitchen with amphitheatre style seating looking down onto the kitchen benches. All the blokes from the burbs sat next to each other on one side of the theatre seating and all the chicks on the other side. What a disaster.

Margery was our host for the evening, but we were allowed to call her Marge. I think Marge may have needed a briefing on why we were all there, and that was to find a life-long partner so we could cook happily ever after together. But poor Marge was more concerned about her cooking utensils and how Garry her servant hadn't laid anything out correctly. I could see Garry might chop off one of Marge's fingers if she wasn't careful and we all might ask for a refund if no one got laid… I mean if no one got a date.

Thankfully, on cue, the waiter came around again to fill up our glasses and we tried our best to get into the evenings event. At one point, my girlfriend and I looked at each other and wondered if Marge had had a few beverages herself, as she kept dropping things and asking poor Garry to pick them up or wash them or replace them. It was quite comical. Fortunately, the organiser came in and stopped Marge momentarily and gave us an introduction to the evening, saying that once Marge had finished the instructions, we were to go down and help, boy-girl-boy-girl style so we got to mingle with the opposite sex. Finally! We didn't come out on this cold blustering evening to be cooked at for 120 bucks.

A few dropped bowls later and entree was ready to be attacked from any direction with boy-girl-boy-girl style. Everyone scrambled down the stairs to line up, trying to make sure they were standing next to their potential cooking partner for life. I was here to support my girlfriend so I asked her if she had noticed any of the suburban types that she might be interested in cooking with. Apparently, she had, as she had raced down the stairs and stood like a kid at school vying for the attention of the guy next to her. I followed her and on passing grabbed another champagne.

Now Marge couldn't be heard over everyone talking to their new friends whilst they helped knead the dough for the gnocchi. Clearly, whoever I was meant to cook with for the rest of my life hadn't arrived yet as there was an odd number, which Marge was quite happy to point out. Luckily, my girlfriend knew that the guy she had stood next to she knew wasn't my type so she offered to include me in on the kneading of the gnocchi. Nice gesture but I was fine sipping on my champagne watching all of this unfold.

There was a mixed bag amongst us all. A few nerdy guys who were useless in the kitchen, and a few chicks who had clearly had far too much to drink, goodness this wet weather really brought out the heat in everyone. I wasn't sure Marge had thought through the entree and her demonstration of how to roll out the gnocchi and then slice it. I think this just made the class go even crazier towards each other.

Thankfully, we were saved by poor Garry who then had to cook all our gnocchi which meant it was time for a short exercise to get to know our new friends before we sat and ate our entree. We all had to stand around one of the kitchen benches and hold a utensil... dear god, I couldn't imagine what we were meant to do with this, and I don't think Marge had any idea either. We were all trying to be polite and not start inappropriate actions with the utensils when the organiser stepped in and gave us our task which was to pair up with two girls and two guys and build something with our utensils. Shoot me now. My girlfriend was really into it, so I had to try and pretend I was too. The guy she liked motioned for us to join him and his mate who had already hooked up with another chick, which was fine by me because he wasn't my type and nor was she.

The exercise proved to be very fruitful in showing my girlfriend that neither of these two guys were potential future cooking partners with their aggressive dictatorship in leading us to build an object. Our group nearly had an argument and both ladies (excluding me as I said I'd just observe) decided to stand up for themselves, which was a huge mistake as this just fuelled the guys even further. At one point, it looked as if these utensils would be used as a weapon. Enter the organiser who had to remind us that this was a get to know you session and was meant to be fun. All I could think was, where's the gnocchi Garry!!

My girlfriend grabbed me and told me to take her away from these two suburban guys and get her a top up of her drink, which was timely as I had sucked mine dry after witnessing that cluster.

"Ladies," said the waiter, who I hadn't noticed before but seemed to have a sparkle in his eye and a mischievous smile.

"Oh, yes please, fill us both up," I begged. The gorgeous waiter started asking us how we were enjoying our night, and if I might add, with a little flirtatiousness and a cheeky grin. My girlfriend launched into the fact that the two guys over there were a complete disaster and that she would pursue new talent for the main course. The waiter turned and looked at me and asked me who I was interested in. I told him I was the plus one and that the organiser couldn't count her way out of a barrel, so the only interest I had was in my glass being full to the brim. With that I winked at him and walked off to taste test some of the gnocchi.

Clearly, Garry was angry because the gnocchi was overcooked like bullets (lucky someone else found this out before anyone broke their teeth). Marge must have been on a time limit, because suddenly we were hurried into the kitchen to help with main course with a new partner. One of the creeps from entree came up to me and said that I looked lonely so he'd be felt obliged to cook with me for main course. I thanked him for his generosity but suggested the lady in the pink cardigan was desperate for his company. He seemed disappointed to have to cook with the lady in the pink cardigan who looked like she would be a virgin.

As main course dragged on, Marge was losing her ingredients and her measurements. Fortunately for me my new friend the waiter had taken pity on me and had decided to help me with my champagne re-filling situation. I think he was flirting with me and so I replied.

CHAPTER 42

BRAINSTRUST

Stephanie Thompson
To: Penny Curtis
Re: Brainy-art

Well, we could have placed a bet on the fact that this was never going to get past the first date mark! What were you thinking?

Penny Curtis
To: Stephanie Thompson
Re: Brainy-art

Oh, thanks very much, you keep telling me to be open-minded….

I should have known from his initial online messages that he wasn't for me. But I admit, I was intrigued if someone so intelligent could meet his yang. And in the back of my mind, I can hear Stephanie and her husband saying to me that I need to be more open-minded and date people that weren't my type.

Enter exhibit A.

Mr Neurosurgeon was probably not my typical type, but his intelligence drew me in. So much so, I decided to get involved to prove to him that I, too, was intelligent. Now, I am going to confess, yes, okay, I may have used a dictionary at times to respond to his online messages, as half of them I did not understand. He used huge words I'd never heard of before, and at times, poetry. I never extended my smarts to the poetry because, let's face it, the only poetry I knew was from Dead Poet's Society and I didn't think it appropriate to recite that to encourage him into a first date, but then again…

My big words back at him encouraged him enough to finally ask me out on a date. Part of me was a little disappointed (I was enjoying throwing big words back at him, half of which I didn't even know how to use in a sentence). But then I was proud of myself as my big words had impressed him enough for a date.

He suggested the Museum of Contemporary Art on early Saturday afternoon. Panic set it. A quick google of their website and a first terrible discovery the bar doesn't serve alcohol until 6pm, then a second terrible discovery that I had no clue who the current artist showing was. Another Google search, this one of the artist, showed that they had written a book, so I purchased it online to read before Saturday.

Look, I like art, but I'm not one of those people who stand and stare at a painting for hours on end. So, I skimmed through the pages and at least had an understanding of the artist's upbringing, which if you ask me was quite contemporary, or should I say, handed to him on a silver spoon, no judgements. If you asked me, I would say they were a very angry personality as seen through their crazy art.

Armed with my new knowledge of this artist and a few big words I'd memorised, I met Mr Neurosurgeon out the front of the MCA. He was nervous as all get out and sweating profusely. I tried my best to encourage him that we were going to have a terrific afternoon together which seemed to relax him a little. Apparently, I was his fourth date. Luckily, he explained I was the fourth date in his life, because if he had meant that day I would have ended it then and there.

I tried to make him feel better, saying, "Well, if it makes you feel any better, you're my first neurosurgeon."

He smiled.

As we entered the museum, I proceeded to reception and said that we were here to buy tickets for the Zebartian collection.

"Oh yes, lovely, wait one moment. Um, unfortunately that collection was moved out last night as it has ended, I'm afraid. Is there another collection you'd be interested in seeing?"

Aghast, I was paralysed.

"I'm sorry, no, this can't be. I was on your website, and it said the Zebartian collection was on?"

The receptionist wasn't in the mood for my antics, and by now I was sweating almost as much as Mr Neurosurgeon next to me.

He pulled me aside and explained that he would be happy to walk around with me and view any collection. In my head I was screaming a long noooooooooooo because I'd done all my due diligence on the Zebartian collection and had no knowledge of anything else. This was a disaster. Who moves a collection? Politely, I smiled at the neurosurgeon and agreed that it would be truly magnificent to walk around with him a view any of the collections. I may have told a white lie at this point, saying I was disappointed as I had studied Zebartian at University. He gave me a puzzled look.

Well, if I couldn't view the artwork I had prepared for, I was definitely going to need a coffee to get me around this show. We ordered coffee for me and a green juice for him. Then we were off to our first collection.

I had no idea who they were, so I read the first plaque that thankfully explained the artist and why they painted the collection. Got it, right. Next painting. Another plaque, another update on what the painting was about. Tick, move onto the next. But when I looked around, there was my sweaty mate still at the first painting. Oh no, has he got stage fright?

"Are you ok?"

He was startled. Maybe he's had a stroke?

"Ah, this piece is just breathtaking, don't you think?"

"I guess, but you should see the crazy piece in the next room, it's nuts."

He gave me a puzzled look.

I was in the third room when I turned around to see if was behind me or still in the second room. Nope, he was still in the first room. I asked him how I was supposed to get to know him if he was too busy staring at the artwork. I asked if he was going to continue like this at every painting.

He asked if I had a problem with that. I said yes. Neither of us compromised, so I left Mr Neurosurgeon staring at the artwork while I continued through the collection to the end and walked out.

Thankfully, it was a beautiful day, and I knew a few girls were at the Opera Bar, so I popped down for a drink. After a glass of champagne, I received a text message from Mr Neurosurgeon, correcting me on the fact I could never have studied Zebartian at University because it's only recent works.

Chapter 43

Textationship

Penny Curtis
To: Stephanie Thompson
Re: Texting Tatts

Some men just need to grow up and not hide behind a text.

Stephanie Thompson

To: Penny Curtis
Re: texting tatts

I agree, if the text is longer than a sentence then call.

Penny Curtis

To: Stephanie Thompson
Re: texting tatts

Hard to call when you're out of credit.

Sometimes you know that you shouldn't waste your time pursuing something you're not remotely interested in, but you pursue it anyway.

Enter the endless text messenger. It absolutely kills me. A few texts are okay but then I want a phone call, or even better a video call – preferably with your clothes on unless you're a model, and then maybe I'll make an exception to the rule.

This endless text mate pushed me over the edge in the end. I mean, if it's not a warning sign that the guy couldn't pick-up the phone or organise his way out of pre-paid Telstra card… Finally, I gave him an ultimatum, even though I wasn't remotely interested at this stage, that if he didn't meet me for a coffee on Sunday morning then I would be deleting his number.

We met Sunday morning for a coffee. There was something about this guy I wasn't sure of, plus I wasn't really interested in him anyway, so there was no way I was meeting him anywhere near my neighbourhood. I decided to go over a bridge or two so that this encounter could not be witnessed by anyone I knew. Of course, I told Stephanie just in case I didn't come back after my coffee but no one else.

I have to admit, I could have thought of a number of other decent things to do rather than sitting at this cafe waiting for Endless Texter. I positioned myself well in the cafe so I could see out to the cars and people walking both sides of the road, but I was also near the toilets which was near the exit.

And there he was, the Endless Texter, walking in like he owned the place. But more significantly what was he wearing? No, wait. Hang on a minute. Oh Jesus Mary and Joseph, what? Has he just escaped prison? Because he had a neck full of tattoos.

His name was Brett.

"Thought you might have just texted, instead," I said. He didn't find any humour in that. We ordered our coffees, and Brett mentioned he'd never been in this "neck of the woods" before, and he "had ta look it up". Sometimes I think I should go with my original instinct from the beginning. Anyway, I had to brace myself for one coffee and then it would be over with.

Our coffees arrived but the conversation sort of didn't. He opened with the infamous question, "Have you ever been out with anyone before with a tattoo?"

Hmmm, how do I answer that politely? In fact, a good friend of mine has a tattoo that looks like a blemish which covers as scar, so yes, I have.

Trying to get the conversation going was painful, and my coffee wasn't strong enough to help me through. I wasn't remotely attracted to Brett, nor did we have anything in common.

Sitting in awkward silence except when Brett slurped his coffee, then he pointed to his fingers. Raising my eyebrows, I shook my head and suggested, laughing, that they were angry because they couldn't text? Brett was not laughing. Not because he didn't find it funny, but because he had no idea I was taking the piss out of him and his texting habit.

"No," he exclaimed, "this tattoo, want to know what it means?"

In my head I wanted to say, "not really," but then my mouth decided polite me was in the house, so I nodded for a yes. Why not, we had nothing else to talk about. Half an hour later, we'd covered the tragic stories of ex-partners whom he had had tattooed on his arms – but then they'd left him and the kids. He seemed to sob a little when he finished telling me about his arm tats.

So far, there were seven partners on his arms with ten kids. Oh dear, I need to get out of here before Brett thinks I'm one of his tattoos. I wanted to as if these were all from prison, but I refrained. Apparently, he had many more stories – but I didn't want to know about them.

Brett seemed confused because he was having a great time. He had no awareness. He forgot that he was on a first date. He didn't understand that hearing about his arm tattoo stories was boring, so hearing about the rest of his body's tattoos sounded doubly boring – so, no.

Bizarrely as we paid the bill, Brett ask me if I wanted to go and get a tattoo.

"Mmm. You know what, I have to be honest, I don't want to take things any further. It was really lovely meeting you and I wish you every success in finding what you want."

Brett seemed dumbfounded. "But you listened to my arm tattoo stories, I thought we'd hit it off. Don't you want to hear the rest of the stories about all my other tatts, babe?'

I was about to say, "Don't babe me," but in my mind I could see him killing me in broad daylight.

"That's okay, sometimes things don't seem what they are." I walked to my car.

Sure enough, I soon received a barrage of text messages by Endless Texter, but none seemed too worrying that he was coming after me, so I kept his number for a few days and then blocked him.

Chapter 44

Expensive Dinner

Penny Curtis
To: Stephanie Thompson
Re: Dinner Tab

Wish I had have seen this one coming.

Stephanie Thompson
To: Penny Curtis
Re: Dinner Tab

Seems to me he was an expert at doing this so I don't think you possible could have seen it coming.

Penny Curtis
To: Stephanie Thompson
Re: Dinner Tab

He seemed so genuine.

I thought I was on the right track with this one. I named him Dissa – it's short for disappointment. We'd already achieved two separate drink catch-ups and he was good fun. A friend who is like a brother to me even met him and thought he seemed like a top bloke.

Dissa suggested our next catch up should be a romantic dinner. He said to leave it to him, and all I had to do is turn up to the restaurant. Though the week we had some funny text exchanges, and he called one night to let me know where he booked dinner.

Wow. A third date in one of the most expensive restaurants in Sydney? This was a red flag. I tried to convince him that perhaps we should save this restaurant for a special occasion, but he was adamant that this was where we should dine.

I was budgeting for a home deposit, and this was the week it was going to take a nosedive if we were going to split the bill.

Even as I arrived at the restaurant, something felt a little off. Got to love that gut instinct. Dissa was already at our table and apparently on his third beer.

It started with pre-dinner drinks. Dissa decided that cocktails were in order. Now, don't get me wrong, I absolutely love a fancy restaurant, however, when you pay $30 a cocktail and it turns up in a tiny, convoluted fancy teacup, it becomes a little less about the cocktail and more about how much more alcohol can I get a hold of to get me through this night.

Entree arrived on a massive white plate with a piddly piece of king fish on it. Dissa had decided to order a few share plates, all of which didn't fit on the table because the plates were too big. In the back of my mind, I was trying my hardest not to add up the price of each plate. Or the fact Dissa had decided to order a glass of wine as a tasting to match each dish.

Dissa had a complete charm to him, but I wasn't fooled. Something was not stacking up. Main course was a sharing plate of duck with side servings of duck fat potatoes and green beans. Dissa ordered a bottle of red which the waiter came out to decant. I was happy with the $80 bottle of un-decanted wine not the $140 bottle of red.

By this stage, I was beginning to get a little suspicious if he had an eating or drinking disorder. The dessert menu arrived, and you guessed it, Dissa ordered some sticky wine. We had to wait a little for my dessert as the kitchen had to twice cook it (probably had to go out buy the ingredients).

But sitting there, talking with Dissa, I really started to fall for his charm and compliments. Who was this gorgeous guy that had me sitting on top of cloud nine, on our third date in one of Sydney's most expensive restaurants?

As our sticky wine came to the table, Dissa needed the men's room, and I sat back and took in the scene looking out across the Sydney Harbour as well as watching the other patrons in the restaurant, most of whom looked like they ate here on a regular basis and knew what to order.

The waiter brought out our dessert, so I waited for Dissa to return, slowly sipping on my dessert wine, eager to try my chocolate molten pudding. I thought maybe Dissa was a little blocked up after all the food we'd eaten and copious amounts of alcohol he had consumed. I thought that he had started on the beers before I arrived, so there was no harm in tasting my hot, oozy dessert.

I'd finished my dessert, and there was still no sign of Dissa. His dessert was just sitting there starring back at me. The waiter came over and checked everything was okay. *Of course, yes thank you.* I finished my sticky dessert wine and sat there. Should I message him? If he's on the toilet that might be awkward. I'll just be patient and wait. He knew his dessert was on its way.

Then another waiter came up to the table with a bottle of champagne, already uncorked. I stopped him and asked what this was for. He explained it was compliments of the gentleman who I'd been dining with. He apparently had to leave suddenly and wanted to send a lovely (expensive) bottle of Veuve to the table as he knew how much I loved French Champagne. I wasn't sure if I was to say thank you as I was alarmed.

In shock, or maybe embarrassment, I called Dissa. Naturally, it went straight through to message bank. I sent a text message asking him what he was thinking and was he coming back?

I had had enough of this evening. With my guts churning, I politely asked the waiter for the bill and sure enough, Dissa didn't disappoint. He had left without contributing a cent to the bill. Looking through the items, it seemed Dissa had a few mates join him for pre-dinner date drinks that were on the bill too.

Feeling sick as I tapped the credit card over the machine, while the sympathetic waiter wrapped up Dissa's dessert, put a stopper in the champagne bottle, and packaged it up for me to take home.

Chapter 45

FOUR

Stephanie Thompson
To: Penny Curtis
Re: Four

Remember, I've told you before, you and sport don't mix!

Penny Curtis
To: Stephanie Thompson
Re: Four

I know, but I have always dreamt of having my partner play golf with me.

Stephanie Thompson
To: Penny Curtis
Re: Four

Yes, keep dreaming, he's out there you deserve better.

I love golf. You could put me anywhere in the world, give me a set of golf clubs no matter the conditions… hang on a minute, erase that and add with no lightening… and I would be in my happy place. My family also loved playing golf and I have a few girlfriends who also like a hit. In my ideal scenario, the man of my dreams would be interested in golf – and not just a hit then calling it a day.

Working ridiculous hours at an Ad Agency was nearly killing me, but then we received notification that an indoor driving range had just opened around the corner, and we were offered a discount. A few of the guys and I decided to take our lunch break, which wasn't allowed by our boss, and ventured off to check this new venue out.

Standing in the foyer, it felt like we had just found Nirvana – mood-lit, simulated driving ranges where you could play all over the world and bonus a well-stocked bar. Ticking all the boxes, we all signed up, grabbed a club and had a hit off of nine holes at St. Andrews in Scotland (whilst sipping on a few alcoholic beverages).

Sadly, we needed our jobs, so we were handing back our clubs as one of the golf pros came up for a chat. He clearly played a lot of golf, and I had to admit he caught my attention with his pearly white teeth and nicely fitted white pants with Ralph Lauren belt. I was dreaming he was standing behind me on the golf course helping me perfect my swing when I was punched on the shoulder by my work colleague.

"Sorry, what did you say?" I asked.

It turns out they were handing out promotions, and one of them was to win four lessons with one of their golf pros. Of course, I was in. I filled in my details and we went back to work.

A week later I received an email saying, "Congratulations, you've won 4 lessons with Freddie Houston, 3-time World Champion at the Golf Driving Range."

I couldn't believe my luck! I'd never won a single thing in my life and here I was winner of four golf lessons with someone called Freddie. I hoped it was the gorgeous golf pro we'd met on our first visit.

On Friday afternoon I decided to claim my prize and book in for my first lesson with Freddie. Lucky for me, it was the hot golf pro I fancied (if it wasn't him, I was probably going to give the lessons to one of my work mates).

Freddie was very cool, and once the lesson started there was definitely flirting going on. He was clearly impressed with my golfing ability and encouraged me to continue coming back for my next lessons. Which I did. I had all three remaining lessons within the following week. My boss kept asking me where I was heading on my lunch break, but I just skipped on past, it was illegal to fire me in my lunch break.

After a few weeks, Freddie plucked up the courage to ask me out. Of course, I had been waiting for him to ask. Probably not the most romantic date, but we planned nine holes of golf with a few drinks afterwards. Perfect.

A little windy, it impacted my game, but we were having a great time. And then I began to realise that Freddie had a way with the ladies. On the second hole, he called me by another lady's name. On the third hole, he offered me a line of cocaine – because, he said, isn't that what you nurses do?

"Um, I'm not a nurse, I'm in advertising and I'm not a drug user."

Freddie was very good at talking about his golfing ability and tournaments he'd won which was impressive for a few holes but not the entire date. He was also quite good at dropping the hint at how much money he had won, and that he owned a McMansion in an exclusive suburb. Then he would call me by another lady's name again. When I corrected him, he just smiled. Still, after drinks, he said he'd like to see me again.

To be honest, I wasn't 100% sure, but I could hear Stephanie in my head saying, "be openminded", and maybe poor Freddie had had one too many lessons with a number of different women and how could possibly remember everyone's name? So, I agreed to a second date.

Before our second date I had a few more lessons with Freddie, and he told me more stories about his rags to riches. It was confusing because they seemed to be different stories to the ones when we were out on our first date. A red flag popped up. He even claimed he was part owner in this driving range venture and that they were expanding internationally. It looked like he was going to head it all up. He exclaimed if things worked out between us, he'd be flying me over to join him. Then he called me by the wrong name.

For our second date, we organised for pre-dinner drinks at his house before going out for dinner, so he sent me his address. Goodness, what a palace! I walked up the long set of stairs past a fountain to the double doors which looked very French. Freddie answered and kissed me on the lips – at least this time he got my name right. But a tour of his McMansion threw up more red flags. As we walked past the lounge room toward the kitchen, I could see a few of the family photos in frames and none looked like Freddie. And Freddie had never mentioned he had kids.

Freddie found champagne glasses and threw open the fridge, which looked pretty full for a bachelor. He reached for a bottle of Veuve. Tick – one red flag taken back! But I also noticed a small alcove, like a study nook, with a single mattress, and a doona and sheet crumpled up, like someone had recently slept there. Nearby were Freddie's golf clubs.

It was a lovely evening, so I suggested we sit outside for our drink. Freddie hesitated, but I ignored him and walked toward the patio door. Freddie jumped in front of me and said that it might be a little cold, but it was too late, I was out the door and noticed two things immediately:

(1) Was that a horse coming towards me? And,

(2) OMG! Have I just stepped in shit? What the hell….

It turns out it wasn't a horse but Freddie's dog, Monty, a Great Dane, who he'd never mentioned before in conversation, and yes, I'd just stepped in its shit. In a panic Freddie started shoeing Monty away. Only, I could clearly see Monty's name tag, and his name wasn't *not* Monty. I took off my shoe, and looking up, I noticed mounds of Monty's (not his real name) shit all over the patio.

"Freddie?" I questioned, "are you too busy to clean-up poor Monty's business? The whole backyard is covered in shit."

Speechless, I walked back inside carrying my shit shodden shoe and headed towards the laundry to wash it off. Inside the laundry there were a variety of different clothes sitting in the washing basket. Some looked like kids school clothing and other items looked like women's clothing. Near the sink was a silver circular tray with a couple of lines of coke on it. In all of this kerfuffle, I could hear Freddie call out, but used a different women's name. That's it, something's not right here, and I am not having a bar of it.

Finishing my glass of Veuve I told Freddie that I thought it best we call it a night as he'd best clean up poor Monty's mess. But I said I'd see him for another lesson in the near future. Freddy didn't seem too perturbed by this, but I felt he'd had a few lines before I'd come over.

A few weeks later I was at Christmas function at my friend's golf club. She was up to date with all the Freddie shenanigans that were now well-and-truly over, but for the life of us we couldn't work out what was wrong with him. After our golf tournament and few lovely glasses of Veuve later we sat down for our Christmas lunch, and my friend introduced me to a woman who knew Freddie.

It turns out Freddie does not own anything! He was a failed Institute of Sport Junior Golfer due to his early addiction to cocaine. He sadly had to caddy for his father's friends as he owed a significant amount of money, and he handled the administration at the driving range which was owned by a group in Singapore. But the house and the dog and the different names? Sadly, because he'd taken so much cocaine and been in and out of rehab, his brother's family has taken him in now that their kids are old enough to understand Uncle Freddie is a little unstable.

CHAPTER 46

TEA LEAVES

Penny Curtis
To: Stephanie Thompson
Re: Stalker

Guess what's arrived at work?

Stephanie Thompson
To: Penny Curtis
Re: Stalker

Twelve long stemmed red roses and I note saying 'I love you, marry me?'

Now that would be reason to smile, however this was reason to not.

I finally had a date on the weekend that I had arranged. It was very simple – a Saturday afternoon cup of tea or coffee, short and sweet. It gives you enough time to work out if they've lied with their profile picture, if they can string a sentence together, and if there's any interest. And if not by this stage you've finished your cup of tea and you can politely exit the scene.

Anthony rocked up and had clearly lied about his age. He was less early forties and more like late fifties. Not off to a great start. It proceeded to get worse. Any question he asked me, he analysed my answer, like this. He asked me what I did for work, and did I like it? I answered that I did like it, I was in in advertising. During my answer Anthony interrupted to make a judgement.

"Oh, you raised your voice when you mentioned that, that means you're not a hard worker."

As you could imagine I'd had enough by this stage. At least Anthony was observant enough to realise when I'd finished my pot of tea. He went to order another, and I declined. He was startled and exclaimed, "but we're only just beginning to get to know each other".

My response: "Sorry Anthony, I'm done, and I'll be honest, sometimes your tea leaves just aren't meant to align." And on that note, I left him standing outside the café as I walked home.

By the time I got home I had received eight text messages from Anthony, most of them about why he thought we were a great couple. I felt insulted the entire time I sat in front of Anthony plus I wasn't even remotely attracted to him. I ignored his texts. Which only made him text more, of which I ignored.

The next week at work I receive an email from work's mailroom with the subject line 'delivery'. I make my way down to the mailroom and there's a massive basket filled with T2 tea and a note from Anthony which read: "Hopefully our tea leaves will align one day".

The scariest part was receiving them addressed to me at work. I never mentioned where I worked. I never even gave him my surname.

So, I sent Anthony a text.

Thank you for the unnecessary hamper of T2, unfortunately this has not helped the alignment of any future tea leaves. Please don't contact me.

Of course, this nutcase responds with a text of hope.

I was hopeful this hamper of tea may have helped our situation, please re-consider.

I didn't respond.

A few weeks passed, and an email came from the mailroom stating I had a delivery. After collecting the small envelope, I sat back down at my desk and read the card.

I thought you'd be interested that there's a women's shoe sale on opposite your building. Hoping our tea leaves will align soon. Love Ant.

I send Anthony a text saying:

Contact me again and I will call the Police.'

Fortunately, that was a message Anthony understood.

CHAPTER 47

NOSTRIL LICKER

Penny Curtis
To: Stephanie Thompson
Re: Violated

I'm over dating.

Stephanie Thompson
To: Penny Curtis
Re: Violated

Well with a subject line like that…are you ok?

Penny Curtis
To: Stephanie Thompson
Re: Violated

I think I am still in shock to be honest.

MY NOT SO BRILLIANT DATING CAREER

One of my work colleagues set me up with his friend. Always a little cautious since I have to work with his mate, I was on my best behaviour. His name was Wes and he seemed nice enough.

We had a little banter before our dinner date, and he seemed harmless. Considering past set-ups, I was going to go in with, "Oh, let's just meet for coffee," but he seemed keen to take me for dinner. My work colleague had spoken quite highly of Wes, so I assumed safe territory and if nothing further was to occur at least it could be a refreshing night out with a decent bloke.

We agreed to meet at the restaurant, a little Italian place in Norton Street, at 7pm. It was a lovely night and I saw Wes standing outside waiting for me in his jeans and white shirt with a bottle of wine. We were ushered in and promptly seated. Before the wine was poured the waiter suggested a glass of complimentary champagne to which we agreed, and once arrived the conversation seemed to flow.

After entrée was finished and we had opened the bottle of wine, Wes started telling me about himself, every now and then asking something about me. We seemed to click, which was nice, but there was something I wasn't one hundred percent sure about but I couldn't quite work it out. I was probably overthinking things, so I just let the night flow.

After main course, we finished the win and Wes promptly ordered us a dessert to share along with two glasses of an Italian dessert wine. Feeling quite tipsy, Wes seemed to be able to hold interesting yet quirky conversation, and every once in a while he would put his hand on my arm or my knee, but I just wasn't sure if I was as fond of Wes as he seemed to be of me.

As the dinner concluded the waiter gave us the bill, and Wes made a few comments about how much I had eaten verses him, as well as the alcohol. In the end I couldn't be bothered arguing about who had eaten what, so I said let's split the bill. Wes seemed pleased with himself. I was now on guard.

We walked up to the main road and Wes invited me back to his place for a night cap, but my instinct was to say no. Wes didn't seem too pleased with this, he mentioned he thought we'd had a great night together, and said I agreed however let's leave it at that for tonight and I looked forward to catching up again soon. I went to give Wes a kiss on the cheek, and he grabbed me in a lock around my waist and proceeded to kiss… well, actually not a kiss…it was like a puppy dog lapping up water and not on my lips but my nostrils!

Inappropriate behaviour Wes! Gross! I couldn't break free, I tried to strain my neck away from his nostril licking advances. I managed to get an arm free and put my hand up against his tongue and pushed his face away. He eventually got the hint.

"Sure, you don't want a night cap?" he said, smugly.

Definitely not, I thought. "Tempting, but not on this occasion thanks Wes. Good night." And I hurriedly walked my way to the taxi rank whilst wiping the saliva from my nostrils.

Stephanie Thompson
To: Penny Curtis
Re: violated

You're right, I also feel violated. What a freak. Did you mention Wes to your colleague?

Penny Curtis
To: Stephanie Thompson
Re: Violated

No, I couldn't, because clearly Wes has told him everything went well and that we'll be seeing each other again. He keeps giving me this raised eyebrow smile when he walks past my desk like Wes has told him I am turned on by nostril licking

Stephanie Thompson
To: Penny Curtis
Re: Violated

Well, you need to march over there and give him a raised eyebrow frown back and tell him it's NOT okay to set you up with pervert mates that think nostril licking is a turn on!

Chapter 48

Coach vs Couch

Penny Curtis
To: Stephanie Thompson
Re: Stick to Coaching

I think I need to take up another sport....tennis doesn't seem to be the right choice.

Stephanie Thompson
To: Penny Curtis
Re: Stick to Coaching

But you love your tennis, plus you've been getting some 'free' coaching from that lovely tennis coach.

Penny Curtis
To: Stephanie Thompson
Re: Stick to Coaching

It won't be free any longer, and I'll need to find another coach.

I'd been at my local tennis club for two years when my regular tennis coach went overseas for a holiday. The receptionist suggested I have a lesson with the new tennis coach, Derrick. If we got along well, we could continue, if not they could find me someone else.

So, the following week I meet up with Derrick to have our first lesson. I took a shining to him instantly. He was nice looking, tall, and athletic. He took an interest in my 'unusual' (I call it talented) two forearms, a left and a right. It turns out Derrick is quite helpful with my game, and I book more lessons.

After one of our lessons Derrick asks me if I would be interested in a drink, which I had been secretly hoping for. Trying not to sound too keen, I agree. The drink is as good, if not better than the tennis lessons, and towards the end Derrick says he'd like to take me a movie. I agree. Tennis lessons and dating an athletic male was ticking all my boxes.

Then I pluck up the courage to ask Derrick over for dinner on a school night at my place. He's keen and we organise it for the following Wednesday night after work.

On Wednesday evening I had cooked up a storm to feed my athletic new tennis coach. Derrick arrived, he's bought me a bunch of flowers and a bottle of wine but mentions he doesn't drink – all the more for me! Conversation flows as Derrick demolishes the hors d'oeurves I'd prepared. Finally, we sit up at the dining table and I watch as Derrick, the barbaric, demolishes the mustard encrusted racks of lamb, with his fingers. I'd never seen anything quite like it before. If they needed proof we're from the caveman era then Derrick was a prime specimen. At the beginning I thought it quite manly, but then when he spoke with his mouth full, elbows on the table and wiping anything from his mouth with his sleeve I was beginning to become a little repulsed.

Derrick seemed appreciative of dinner and excused himself from the table to sit down on my couch. I wasn't surprised, after witnessing his mannerisms at the dinner table, that he didn't offer to help clear the plates. I thought I'd give him a rest from food and decided to clean up a little before serving up dessert. I was talking away at him and he had turned on the television, which I didn't think appropriate. It's our first real date together, surely I was more interesting than the ABC?

None-the-less, I continued to clean-up and chat, with the occasional comment of support from Derrick. Washing up in the sink, I heard a noise, like a rustling of a belt, and thought maybe Derrick had gone to the bathroom. As I walked across to the dining table to collect the placemats to wipe down, I suddenly realise Derrick hasn't gone to the bathroom, but instead decided in his caveman style to take his pants down and flip out his appendage on my couch and... started to do something inappropriate to his appendage.

"What are you doing!?!?" I screamed.

Derrick sat bolt right up and had this clumsy look on his face and makes this ridiculous comment: "I thought you'd like a little dessert?"

"Not on my couch, you feral beast, pull your pants up and get out!!" I screamed.

Derrick jumped up and nearly tripped over his pants as I walked around the other side and opened the front door looking outside, not at him.

He tried to kiss me on his way out, but I turned my head.

"I guess you won't want any more tennis lessons from me then?" he asked.

I just raised my eyebrows and said nothing and slammed the door on Derrick.

Stephanie Thompson
To: Penny Curtis
Re: stick to coaching

Don't you give up playing at your favourite club just because a caveman tries to give you dessert on your couch.

Penny Curtis
To: Stephanie Thompson
Re: stick to coaching

Funny, he's actually been asked to leave the tennis club, we all received an email asking anyone with any information to come forward, apparently the barbarian has been giving free coaching and dessert lessons on other ladies' couches.

Chapter 49

Cop That

Stephanie Thompson
To: Penny Curtis
Re: Busted

Did you end up in jail?

Penny Curtis
To: Stephanie Thompson
Re: Busted

No, but came very close though.

Stephanie Thompson
To: Penny Curtis
Re: Busted

You do realise he's a Police Officer and he's just protecting the community?

Penny Curtis
To: Stephanie Thompson
Re: Busted

I get it, but, surely he can make allowances for what could have been his soon to be girlfriend?

Stephanie Thompson
To: Penny Curtis
Re: Busted

Well, I guess, but I think you may have stretched the rules slightly.

After talking my way out of a fine for driving around Sydney with Victorian number plates, the negotiation seemed pretty reasonable – dinner with the Cop. He seemed to have good humour and was also not bad on the eye. Dinner it was. I gave him my phone number and promptly received a call the following day.

Ian (not the type of police name I was thinking) and I met at a horrendous pub in Coogee because we agreed this was halfway, although I suspect it was probably more three quarters his way. Dinner was fun, he had good humour although for some reason I felt like I had to be on my best behaviour.

"Did you drive?" he questioned.

"Yes, but I haven't had a drink yet," I responded. Why did I have to give the drinking bit away so soon?

When Ian walked me to the car, I was waiting for the breathalyser, but fortunately he let me off again, considering

I'd only had a glass of wine with dinner. Once in my car I made sure I put my seatbelt on, turned the lights on, indicated, checked my mirrors, and then drove off carefully. Wiping the sweat from my brow, I received a text from Ian. Was this another test? Was he driving a few cars behind to see if I'd reply to his text whilst driving? Not willing to risk it, I waited, and I texted him back once I'd pulled up at my place.

A few days later Ian was keen to see me again. He mentioned it was going to be a nice day on Saturday and would I like to join him in the afternoon for a stand-up paddle board? Absolutely, I would like that. Driving to his place, it was clear the first date wasn't halfway between us – I managed to find Ian's place half a tank of petrol later. We loaded the boards on top of my car and without thinking I started to reverse without my seatbelt on, over his garden bed and clipped a few bricks off his fence. I pulled up in a panic, staring straight ahead. Casually, Ian said, 'Probably best you put your seatbelt on'. Yes, sir. And then I burst out laughing hysterically, it must have been the guilt inside me. I could barely see because I had so many tears in my eyes. Ian was not laughing.

Thinking my chances were over with Ian, to my relief Ian asked me if I would be interested in another date? He suggested a bike ride around the waterfront the following weekend if I was free.

On the afternoon of the bike riding date, I turned up at Ian's and decided it was safer not to drive into his driveway, but best to park outside on the street. Ian was there pumping up the tyres on the bikes. It was a magnificent day. We set off. Having a background of cycling in Europe whereby they don't wear helmets, and bike riders are respected, I had embraced their attitude and didn't usually wear a helmet.

So off I cycled, helmet-free. There was a loud, deep, "Ehem" from Ian behind me. "Haven't you forgotten something?' he asked and pointed to his head.

What? Is he being serious? How bloody regimental was this guy? It's a beautiful day and we were riding on a BIKE PATH, not on a main road, what could possibly go wrong? Surely, we could negotiate this. Apparently, this was a non-negotiation and Ian said he'd ride the bike back home if I did comply with wearing a helmet. I thought he was joking, to be honest, so I peddled on. Looking back, I saw Ian in the distance heading back home. I thought better of it and put my helmet on and rode back to him.

Unimpressed, Ian told me he couldn't go out with someone who continuously broke the rules.

Fair enough.

Chapter 50

Pomm Fizzle

Stephanie Thompson
To: Penny Curtis
Re: Deuce

OK, I've nearly had enough now, I'm taking you to see a therapist.

Penny Curtis
To: Stephanie Thompson
Re: Deuce

Why?

Stephanie Thompson
To: Penny Curtis
Re: Deuce

How any times do I have to remind you that sport and you shouldn't mix?

There is nothing better than the lead up to a date with a guy you think has potential. Then there's nothing worse when, at the beginning of the date, all the pre-date communication goes to shit because someone made it to the bar before you and promptly drank the beer drum and is now reeking of alcohol and can barely string a sentence together.

Helping him into a taxi to send him home, I decided that pre-first date, Frank* (not his real name) had deposited enough into the relationship bank for me to believe it was just nerves that had got the better of him. What a disaster and how disappointing.

Sheepishly, Frank apologized for his behaviour and suggested he make it up to me by a dinner. Giving him the benefit of the doubt, I decided Frank was worth a second date.

We met outside a restaurant in Paddington and as I got out of my taxi, I saw Frank sucking down tobacco like it was his last meal. He came over and gave me a kiss on the cheek and complimented me how nice I looked. I could smell booze and cigarettes. Frank walked me into the restaurant where waitress seated us and gave us menus. Drinks arrived, and the conversation started to flow a little better the second time around: at least I could understand his words – less slurred.

I was in the middle of a sentence when Frank interrupted that he needed to go for a cigarette. *Sure, knock yourself out.* Off went Frank whilst I sat there with my wine. I was wondering how long he'd be when a potent smog engulfed me, and Frank appeared from within the smoky haze. He absolutely stank of it. Sitting down, he took a gulp of his beer and asked me where we were in the conversation. Thankfully the waiter appeared, and we ordered our meal and another drink. The conversation continued however I was dodging Frank's smoke-filled breath. He didn't seem to be aware.

We were half-way through our meals and mid-topic when, as if on cue, Frank excused himself for another cigarette. Unbelievable, during dinner! I wanted to vomit. While Frank was outside sucking on the last of his cigarette, I ordered myself another drink, might as well try and ease the pain of this.

As Frank sat back down, a hazy blur engulfed the remains of my meal and smoke came out of his mouth as he spoke.

I admit, there was still an attraction there, but it was overshadowed by Frank's constant twitching to go and smoke a cigarette, then his breath when he returned – enough to blow me off my chair. We finished our meal and drinks, settled the bill, and to my surprise Frank asked if I'd like nightcap back at his place which was around the corner.

Why not? Besides the smoking, he was a gentleman. On the five-minute walk home Frank managed to chain smoke three cigarettes. Inside his place, there was a smoke haze subtly drifting near the ceiling above his lounge. As Frank walked past me on his way to organize a bottle of wine and glasses, he leaned in and kissed me, depositing the remaining smoke from his three cigarettes. Frank seemed pretty happy with himself and skipped off to the kitchen.

When he came back and poured the wine, he explained he'd been wanting to kiss me since he met me, but he was too nervous. Poor Frank. A glass of wine later and Frank decides to try his luck with more kissing, to which I oblige since it had been an hour since his last cigarette. It was a nice kiss, and it continued. Soon Frank's hands became involved. His breathing got heavier. Frank seemed to be putting in considerable effort. Frank was definitely in his own world. Frank had a moment. Oh Frank, for God sake's....

Frank jumped up. His chinos where severely stained. Really? That soon? It was just a kiss. Embarrassed, Frank tried hiding the rather large stain down his pants as he walked backwards into the bathroom. He told me he wouldn't be long, then said he'd like it if I stayed for another glass of wine as he slammed the bathroom door shut.

I'd had enough. I finished my wine and walked out the front door, leaving Frank to clean himself up. Fortunately, a taxi with its light on drove past at that moment and I jumped in and did not look back. Luckily, Frank received my message loud and clear.

Chapter 51

Not so Magic Mike

Penny Curtis
To: Stephanie Thompson
Re: The Magician

I took your advice and have avoided any sportsmen, salty men and scientific men.

Stephanie Thompson
To: Penny Curtis
Re: The Magician

Oh, I'm so proud of you! So, tell me how did this date go?

Penny Curtis
To: Stephanie Thompson
Re: The magician

Well, I think we add magicians to the avoid list.

After a few months recovering from a severe shoulder injury, I decided, because I could now walk, I could date again. I went back online with positive affirmations that I deserved to meet someone wonderful.

Scrolling through, one guy caught my attention, he looked fit and fun. I reached out to him, and we matched. A few online conversations later and we organised to meet up for a walk at a local park. I explained that I was still recovering from my broken shoulder and that I'd be wearing a sling and couldn't power walk.

At the gates where we were meeting, I couldn't see him, so I sent him a test.

"Turn around," he responded. "I'm the guy with the sausage dog."

Turning around, I wasn't sure what to look at first. The sausage dog whose stomach was dragging along the ground or the fit guy I've supposedly met online whose stomach was also dragging along the ground. Neither of them looked like their online profiles.

We started our walk. He was very confident. He started talking about himself. A quarter of the way around the park we bumped into his mother and her neighbour, who were also walking the park. He introduced me as his date. It was awkward. But what was more awkward was the fact that halfway round the park we bumped into his aunty and her friend walking around the park.

Did he deliberately set up our walk so I'd meet his whole family by the time we'd finished one lap?

He continued to talk about himself the entire way round the park. I'm not sure if my shoulder was hurting or I'd had enough of this bloke. I was concerned for his sausage dog who seemed out of breath and could barely walk. We finally stopped at the gates where we started, and he was keen for another lap. I quickly indicated that my shoulder was a little sore and that I would pass.

Clearly, this guy wasn't one for taking no, so he suggested a drink back at his place. I'll pass on that option too, thanks very much. As I go to shake his hand and thank him for the walk, he tells me I can't leave without seeing his magic trick.

"You do like magic, don't you?"

In my mind I wanted to respond, "If the magic does abracadabra and gets me out of this situation and home, yes." In fact, I am not a fan of magic. I'm not sure why, maybe it was a clown at a birthday party, but I really don't enjoy magic. It turns out this guy was a magician. Here we go. I oblige.

Standing at the corner of a busy area, he pulled out a box of cards from his oversized hoodie that had a stench like it hadn't been washed for a few months. He shuffled the cards and told me to pick a card. I picked a card, he took it back without looking at it, then tried to distract me by telling me to look at his dog as he continued to shuffle the cards. Whilst one of my eyes looked at his poor dog, my other eye keeps on the prize, and I saw him put my card into his hoodie side pocket. I didn't say anything. He then waved his hand over all the cards, flicked them, clapped them together, then quickly tried to distract me further and as he quickly pulled my card out of his hoodie, put it back into the pack, then magically snapped it out and said, "There you are, was it a Queen of Hearts?"

Unimpressed, I said I saw him put my card in his hoodie pocket. He claimed he didn't. I wasn't going to have an argument with this magician who seemed to be a little bit of a liar. So, I thank him for the walk and his magic trip and walked back to my car. He called after me saying he had another magic trick to show me. I kept going.

> Abracadabra,
> Diddly woo.
> You seem like a nutter,
> I'm definitely not for you.

Chapter 52

BARRY WHITE

Penny Curtis
To: Stephanie Thompson
Re: Barry White

This was definitely one out of the box or the 'funny' farm.

Stephanie Thompson
To: Penny Curtis
Re: Barry White

I love Barry White's famous song, please tell me he sang it to you? Was he a good singer?

Penny Curtis
To: Stephanie Thompson
Re: Barry White

I was mortified enough, signing would have made things even worse.

I should have read the early warning signs, but sometimes I get a little carried away and enjoy their crazy. Right from the word go this guy was full of himself. Not once did he really listen to what I had to say, and when he did, it was to tell me otherwise.

Let's call him Charlton, it sounds right up his pompous ally. Our initial conversations over the phone went like this. He did all the talking, and every now and again I would give some input. "Oh really?" or "I agree". Charlton, apparently, had a huge wine collection, a whole room downstairs that he built with his own hands, but because his ex-wife got the house it turns out he couldn't take the room with him. Poor Charlton.

Charlton liked his wine. Every conversation was about wine. I sometimes entertained myself and changed the topic, but sadly Charlton didn't understand anything… but wine.

I agreed to dinner. We agreed to meet for a pre-dinner drink at a pub across the road from the French restaurant he has booked for us. I was a little early, so I order a cocktail and grabbed a table. Scanning the room, I thought to myself that if dinner went south I would head back here as there was some great fresh meat at this place.

When I look towards the door, my margarita nearly came out through my nose as I gasped at the guy walking towards me.

Is it? No, it can't be, I think it's Barry White! He's wearing an off-mustard-coloured turtleneck skivvy with a full white pants and jacket suit. I couldn't help myself as he leaned in to give me a kiss on the cheek.

"You didn't tell me it was fancy dress!"

Clearly, Charlton didn't get my humour and went off and got himself – Barry White II – a drink. I skolled my margarita and pointed at my empty glass for Barry to get me another. Then I sunk down into my chair as the 'fresh meat' were looking at my sugar daddy in disbelief. Who would wear such an outfit? I could definitely say that, quoting Barry's line, "I can't get enough of your love, baby…" would NEVER happen with Barry White II.

Barry returned from the bar and was on autopilot speaking about wine again. I couldn't help myself, I threw out random useless untruthful facts about wine regions and wines keeping a poker face, whilst Barry questioned me on my facts. All lies, Barry!

Barry had finished his drink. I had not. Barry suggested we walk across to the restaurant as our booking was now. He didn't understand that I hadn't finished my drink. He didn't care. But I cared, so I skolled my second margarita, praying one of the fresh meat blokes would grab me by the arm before I walked out, and pull me in close and Barry walked off into the distance. Unfortunately, that dream did not happen.

So, Barry said this French restaurant was the best in Sydney. I disagreed. Barry had also suggested prior to this dinner that we'd play a game – oh, goodie – and that game was that we each purchase a bottle of wine that would suit the restaurant and make sure the label was covered so at dinner we could each guess what type of wine it was and what region it was from. Wow! This dinner was just getting better.

It was like a scene with Manuel out of Fawlty Towers. Our lovely French waiter who could barely speak English went to grab the wine and was about to pull it out of the brown paper bag when Barry White's hand came from nowhere and grabbed

Chapter 53

Fast Food

Penny Curtis
To: Stephanie Thompson
Re: 280 caloriemeters later

Remind me next time I meet someone online, I am NOT that desperate to cross borders.

Stephanie Thompson
To: Penny Curtis
Re: 280 Caloriemeters Later

I tried warning you, but you were adamant, how bad could it have been?

Penny Curtis
To: Stephanie Thompson
Re: 280 Caloriemetres Later

Firstly, I got stuck in peak hour traffic out of Sydney.

Stephanie Thompson
To: Penny Curtis
Re: 280 Caloriemetres Later

Well, I did try and tell you to leave earlier, but you decided to go straight after work whereby all people are trying to start their weekend.

Penny Curtis
To: Stephanie Thompson
Re: 280 Caloriemetres Later

Well, that's six hours I'm never going to get back in my life, plus it was literally a two hour date and I was back in Sydney before midnight.

Stephanie Thompson
To: Penny Curtis
Re: 280 Caloriemetres Later

Oh dear, that doesn't sound promising….what happened?

People tell you to be open minded, to think outside the square. So, I did, so much so I crossed borders for a date with a Canberrian. Clearly the peak hour traffic from Sydney to Canberra should have screamed alarm bells but in the back of my head I can hear everyone saying: "Oh, it's when you least expect it."

Finally, I got to Canberra and messaged my date that I had arrived, I was heading to the bar and would meet him there. He seemed lovely online and on the couple of pre-date phone calls we had, so at this stage it all seemed good.

He was late, nearly an hour. I had downed my first drink and was ordering my second when he arrived without an apology. So, that was warning sign number three. It's usually three strikes and you're out but because I'd driven all the way to Canberra, I thought I'd give him the benefit of the doubt and continued.

Sitting at the bar, he bought his own drink, and I bought mine. The conversation wasn't great, his attention span was that of a peanut. It was as if he'd used up all his conversation online or over the phone to me. He added no value whatsoever to the conversation. He kept looking around the room, as if distracted. At one point, he excused himself and went off to the toilet, and I caught him as he came out of the toilet walking over to a group of people and sitting down to talk with them.

I was left at the bar by myself. Not a good sign in my book. So, I ordered myself another drink and waited. Every now and then I turned to see him talking to the other group, although they didn't seem interested in his company. Eventually, Canberra either remembered he had a date sitting at the bar or got the hint that the other group weren't interested in his small talk. He came back and sat down. I questioned who they were (not the fact he'd ditched me and didn't have the decency to tell me where he was going). Apparently, it was his ex-girlfriend and her new boyfriend and some of their mutual friends. Was he serious? Points – minus 5 at this stage.

He was hungry, so was I, so he suggested we grab a bite. At this point I thought I could go it alone as I had checked out. But then I had no idea where I was in Canberra, nor did

I know any restaurants. We walked through the streets, and he made useless comments about random facts of nothing. By this stage I didn't really care. We stopped at a few restaurants, he read out the menu, looked at me and then as I said, "yes, that sounds nice let's try it," he walked on.

We walked and walked. My feet were hurting, and I was hungry. He said dinner wasn't far – just around the corner, then just one more. I kept pointing out restaurants.

"Nah," was his reply. Eyeroll yours truly and more points lost for him.

Then as we came around a corner, he walked straight through the doors at Hungry Jacks. (Insert my largest deer in headlight eyeball eyes with an expletive!!)

No way, are you kidding me? I'm not sure why I walked in but when I did, he had already placed his order. I asked him politely if this was some sort of a joke. He just stared blankly through me, either he did not understand, or he clearly couldn't give a crap.

The next thing I heard was the Hungry Jack's employee asking me what I'd like to order.

"Just a taxi driver back to Sydney right now, thank you."

He looked back at me politely and said, "Ma'am, if you're not going to order do you mind moving to one side so I can serve the next person in line."

And with that, I drove back over the border.

Chapter 54

Tinder-National

Penny Curtis
To: Stephanie Thompson
Re: *Oui* means pee?

How's technology these days?

Stephanie Thompson
To: Penny Curtis
Re: *Oui* means pee?

I think it's incredible to be honest. I can track the whereabouts of my husband and he doesn't even know!

I had a wonderful trip to France with my gorgeous parents. We were very busy and becoming accustomed to the European way of life – including an afternoon siesta then a late dinner, which was just perfect. I'd pack Mum and Dad off to their hotel wishing them *bonne notte* (goodnight) and

I would race off to check my mobile for any potential dates with a hot European male so I could fall in love.

The only problem, I didn't speak French. By the time I interpreted their message in Google Translate, I was in the next town. Boy, it was exhausting.

But on one occasion, we were staying in town a few extra days. I turned on my online dating app, and up popped a nice-looking man who had 'liked' my profile. It must have been a sign. He said he has broken English, and I told him I spoke broken French – what a perfect match. Feeling that my stars had aligned, I waved *bonne notte* to Mum and Dad who were staying in a five-star luxury hotel and trotted off to my one-star AirBnB. Tonight, I was meeting Pierre at a rooftop bar in the middle of the city. I sent my 'safety text' to Steph in case this was my last night on earth…

Not the easiest rooftop bar to navigate to, but then again, nothing in France was easy. However, once I found the place, I was blown away by the atmosphere and the view. Definitely a place to bring my parents tomorrow night (should I survive).

Pierre appeared and, thankfully, looked exactly like his photos. The only issue was that his 'broken English' was very broken (more like he'd had a stroke even trying to say hello), and my French was worse. There was a lot of smiling and a lot of silence in the beginning. Somehow, I worked out that he was the coach of the French Olympic Swim Team, which I was very impressed with.

Then I had a brainwave! Even though it cost me a fortune. I turned the personal hotspot on my iPhone so we would use the Google Translate app! Well, what a great feat that was. And Pierre took to it like swimmers take to pool lates. We exchanged one Google Translate after another. He was a slow typer, but we persisted, and we were enjoying it.

But after two drinks it was becoming exhausting, so I used the excuse that I had an early start in the morning.

Pierre, however, was adamant that the night was still young. He offered to take me on his Vespa up to the lookout "just up there" – and when in France, why not.

We hopped on Pierre's Vespa. I'd had a few drinks now, and I was sure that the Frenchs Swim Team Coach wouldn't want to be seen in the papers for mugging or killing a foreigner, so I was sure I was safe. We rode up the mountain with the city lights behind us, and before long we were at the lookout. It was postcard perfect.

Standing in Pierre's muscular arms, I began planning out our wedding in my head. Me learning French, teaching our French children English, travelling the world together as he collected more and more Olympic medals for his swimmers.

I was quickly snapped out of it when I realised Pierre must have read my mind. Suddenly, he was down on one knee, holding my hands and looking up at me.

"Oui?" he said, pointing at each of us in turn.

Freaking out completely, I pretended I didn't understand a word he was saying and politely tried to indicate I needed to pee. Unfortunately, after 5 years of learning high-school German, I was mixing my words up. "Toiletten?" with a bit of Italian "Cia?".

Poor Pierre looked sad and confused at the same time. I, on the other hand, needed to get out of there quick sticks.

As I launched myself off the back of Pierre's Vespa outside my AirBnB, he once again tried to get down on one knee and kiss my hands. "Oui?"

Bonjour, Pierre, a lovely night, but I have to pee. Bonne notte.

And with that I was off up the driveway.

Safely back in my apartment, I heard my phone beep. It was Pierre, explaining how much he loved me and that his proposal still stood.

Chapter 55

Heart Attack

Penny Curtis
To: Stephanie Thompson
Re: O.M.G

Can I start that weekend again?

Stephanie Thompson
To: Penny Curtis
Re: O.M.G

You have to tell me everything, how was the wedding?

Penny Curtis
To: Stephanie Thompson
Re: O.M.G

It sort of went wrong right from the very beginning…

Stephanie Thompson
To: Penny Curtis
Re: O.M.G

Oh, I love it, what happened?

I was ecstatic to receive an invite to a close girlfriends wedding, I'd known her and her fiancé for many years.

On the day of the wedding, my flatmate offered to give me a lift to the church. She gave me a thumbs up on my outfit and she said I looked 'smokin', so with an air of confidence we jumped in her car and took off.

To paint the picture clearly, we were in my flatmate's car and I read her the Church address. She's indicated that she knows it already as it's the church she went to with her grandparents when she was younger. Our confidence was oozing. But as we rounded the corner, we saw the bridal car. Panic! So, my flatmate drove up behind the church and dropped me off, telling me to run into 'that door' which would have me sitting in the middle section of the church. I said thanks, bolted out of the car and into the side door into the church. Inside, I grabbed my seat next to a lovely couple, straightened my dress out and patted my hair ready for my girlfriend to walk down the aisle without her knowing I was late. I stretched my neck to see if I could see any of our friends, but the Church was packed.

I could barely see the groomsmen, I thought I recognised a few of her fiancé's friends. I could barely see the groomsmen, but thankfully the organ music started playing and everyone stood up and turned around to see the bride.

I was excited. I got out my handkerchief, just in case. As the bride began walking down the aisle, I took a closer look and realised it wasn't my girlfriend. *Holy cow, I'm in the wrong church!*

As the bride (who I must admit did look lovely though perhaps was borderline a little too botoxed) walked past me, I turned and ducked out the side door.

Turns out I was in the Catholic church – the Anglican Church was on the opposite corner. Jesus Christ.

As I bolted across the road, I saw my friend and her father waiting to enter the Anglican Church. Her father commented, "Isn't it usually the bride that should be late?" I smiled back at them as I bolted inside.

I wasn't the only one who couldn't read the invitation properly. The groom's close mate was also late. We gave each other an understanding look as we snuck in together. I quickly scanned the room – my friends and their partners were all down the front (always on time, I rolled my eyes) so I sat on the pew with the groom's mate. The wedding ceremony was lovely, although I do remember thinking the priest must have smoked something as I'm sure he got the wedding couple's names wrong.

At the reception held at my girlfriend's parent's place, and having a terrific time, the bride tells me I should meet her husband's friend, Justin the farmer. Funnily enough, we had already – it was the guy that turned up late to the church with me. Bless her cotton socks, she dragged me halfway across the dance floor to him. He had some pretty bad dance moves, but at least he was having a go.

There's an instant connection, not because of his dance moves but more because I was late to the church as well, and he offered to take to me for a boogie – nothing like a bit of

"I've had a few too many and I'll show you just how blue my suede shoes are working". There was a bit of flirting, which was nice, then speeches so we went back to our own tables.

After some more music, Justin came over and sat next to me. By now, words are getting a little blurred, but all my friends and their partners are giving me the thumbs up. So, there was a pash. I love a good pash at a wedding. He decided to take it further and asked me if it was too much for a… night cap?

Justin lived in Gippsland, too far for a taxi home, so he had booked a hotel room already. He invited me back to the hotel bar, saying if I didn't think that was too forward of him. I was tipsy and with a hot farmer, so in my mind it was perfect. Nice hotel bar, great atmosphere, we were clearly both attracted to each other and having a great laugh.

The next thing I know, the farmer has hurled me over his shoulder like I am a sheep ready to be shorn and taken me to the lift. But I'm okay with this because the farmer is strong and very manly. Well, I am not sure what happened next, but it appeared that the farmer and the city girl found each other amongst the bedsheets and were enjoying each other immensely.

We were like rabbits all night long.

In the early hours of the morning, I felt a slight stir and the farmer pulled me onto him. Suddenly we were at it again, which built into a raging bull! While I was too busy giving the farmer what for and pretending I was some cowgirl, I looked down to see he had gone white! There wasn't much movement on his behalf, and his eyes start to roll back into his head – which unfortunately I take for being the farmer has just released the lasso. But sadly, the poor farmer has not released his lasso, and instead looks like he's about to die.

I jumped off… in slight panic. Actually, not slight panic. Full panic! I shouted out to the farmer who didn't respond. I checked his pulse, but it was difficult to feel because mine was coming through my chest at a great rate of knots. He was breathing… I think. Very shallow breathing, and he was out cold. Oh my god. I covered him up with blankets and ran for the hotel phone.

I called reception in my 'I'm trying to be calm, but actually panicking voice' and asked them if they could organise an ambulance.

"Ma'am, why do you think you need an ambulance?" asked the guy at reception.

"Because the guy I've just had sex with looks like he's about to die," I blurted. There was silence at the other end (and over in the bed too I might add). The next minute, he confirms the ambulance is on its way.

Meanwhile, the poor farmer comes too, and is in a little shock, as am I. I had no idea what to do. I was running around like a headless chook, all the time speaking to the farmer to make sure he stays alive.

There was a knock at the door. The ambulance has arrived, thank Christ.

Ambulance officer: "What is his name?"

Me: Awkward moment. "Um…I think it's…actually, I can't remember." Christ, I've forgotten his name!

Ambulance Officer: "And what was happening for him to respond like this?"

Me: (Seriously is this guy now just taking the mickey or what.) "Well, um, we met at our friend's wedding earlier today. And we hit it off, and we were having, you know…"

Ambulance Officer: "You were having what? Drugs, or—'

Me: "No, no drugs at all. I mean we've had alcohol. And sex."

The guy from reception is watching, he gives me a look of disgust, rolling his eyes.

Ambulance Officer: "And this only occurred once, for him to respond like this I take it?"

Me: "Um, well, he only responded like this on the last occasion we did it."

Ambulance Officer: "Right, and how many other times?"

Me: "Pretty much all night". By this time I'd gone beetroot red and desperately wanted to escape the interrogation.

The Ambulance Officer and his partner checked all of the farmers vital signs and ran a few serious looking tests. A few more questions, and the farmer was looking very lethargic and pasty white. A little while later, the Ambulance Office advised me that they highly recommend the will be taking my 'partner' immediately to the hospital. Did I want to accompany him?

What?

I felt pretty guilty, but I also felt a little awkward, plus the bed looked quite inviting now the farmer wasn't in it looking like death warmed up. But I took the moral high ground and accompanied the farmer in the ambulance to the hospital. Not a great look, tipsy in a wedding outfit with a bloke I'd forgotten the name off being wheeled into emergency.

After a few hours of tests, the farmer was given his prognosis and allowed to be discharged. I wasn't seeing the funny side of things at that point, however at least the *farmer saw the lighter side of the situation.*

"Well at least that's one way I'd be happy to go."

It turns out the farmer had a hole in his heart and had suffered a mild irregular heartbeat which had set off a tremor... which basically meant he had a heart attack.

Stephanie Thompson
To: Penny Curtis
Re: O.M.G.

HE HAD A HEART ATTACK WHILST YOU BOTH WERE IN THE THROWS OF IT?

Penny Curtis
To: Stephanie Thompson
Re: O.M.G.

Yes.

Stephanie Thompson
To: Penny Curtis
Re: O.M.G.

A HEART ATTACK?????

Penny Curtis
To: Stephanie Thompson
Re: O.M.G.

YES, STEPHANIE, HE HAD A HEART ATTACK.

THE END.

www.ingramcontent.com/pod-product-compliance
Lightning Source LLC
Chambersburg PA
CBHW070642160426
43194CB00009B/1542